FREEDOM AT MIDNIGHT

FREEDOM AT MIDNIGHT

AUSTRIA : 1938-55 A STORY OF THE TRAUMATIC YEARS OF OCCUPATION

Reg Herschy

First published in 1989 by
Reg Herschy
in association with
The Self Publishing Association Ltd
Lloyds Bank Chambers, 18 High Street,
Upton upon Severn, Worcestershire, WR8 0HW

A MEMBER OF

© Reg Herschy 1989
ISBN 1 85421 046 7

This book is copyright. No part of it may be reproduced in any form without permission in writing from the publishers except by a reviewer who wishes to quote brief passages in connection with a review written for inclusion in a newspaper, magazine, radio or television broadcast.

British Library Cataloguing in Publication Data

Herschy, R.W. (Reginald Walter), 1926 –
Freedom at midnight: Austria: 1938-1955: a
story of the traumatic years of occupation.
1. Austria.Foreign occupation by military
forces, 1938-1955
I. Title
943.6'052

ISBN 1-85421-046-7

Typeset by Printit-Now, Upton-upon-Severn
and printed and bound in Great Britain by
Billings and Son Ltd., Worcester

The 6th British Armoured Divisions "first mailed" sign with electrically controlled thumb which gave driver's entering Austria at Thörl Maglern the "thumbs up" sign (9th May 1945).

To my wife who lived under the political systems of Dollfuss, Schuschnigg and Hitler and survived to witness the Allied liberation of her country.

CONTENTS

	ACKNOWLEDGEMENTS	
	INTRODUCTION	13
1	ANSCHLUSS – AUSTRIA UNDER THE SWASTIKA	17
2	FROM THE DESERT TO THE ALPS	29
3	CONFLICT IN KLAGENFURT	53
4	THE DISPUTED FRONTIER	75
5	RESISTANCE	87
6	THE FALL OF VIENNA	105
7	BTA: BRITISH TROOPS IN AUSTRIA	121
8	DENAZIFICATION	141
9	REBIRTH OF A PROUD NATION	159
10	EPILOGUE	175
	BIBLIOGRAPHY	177
	APPENDIX: CHRONOLOGY OF EVENTS	183
	INDEX	189

LIST OF MAPS

AUSTRIA:	Showing international frontiers 1955; Provincial borders 1955; Austro-Italian frontier 1914; Italy-Yugoslav frontier 1939; Plebiscite area 1920	8 & 9
AUSTRIA:	Zones of occupation 1945-55	33
TRIESTE & VENEZIA GIULIA:		55
THE AUSTRIAN EMPIRE	1282-1918	77
PLEBISCITE AREAS:	Carinthia 1920	80
VIENNA:	Districts of occupation 1945-55	118

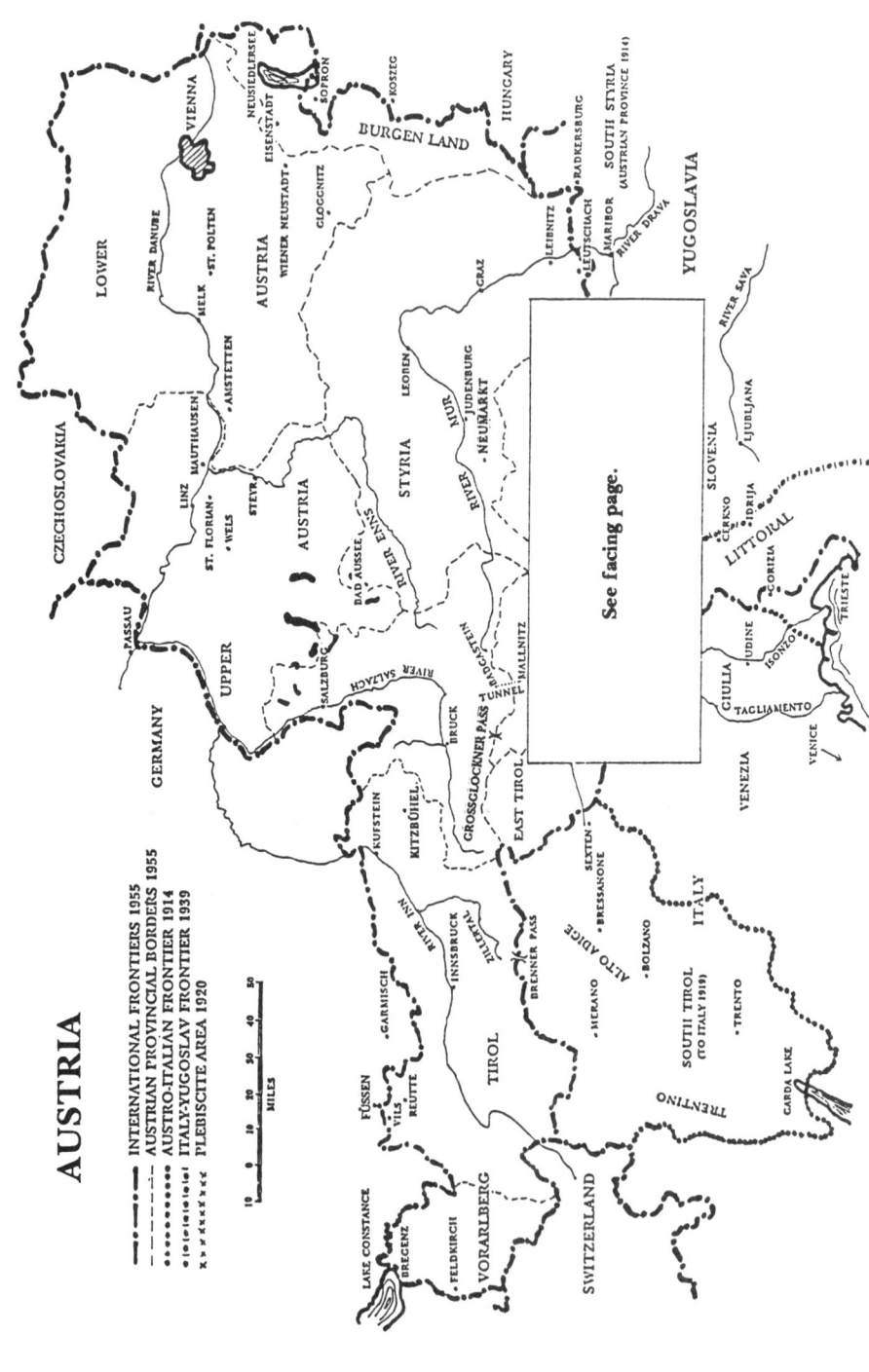

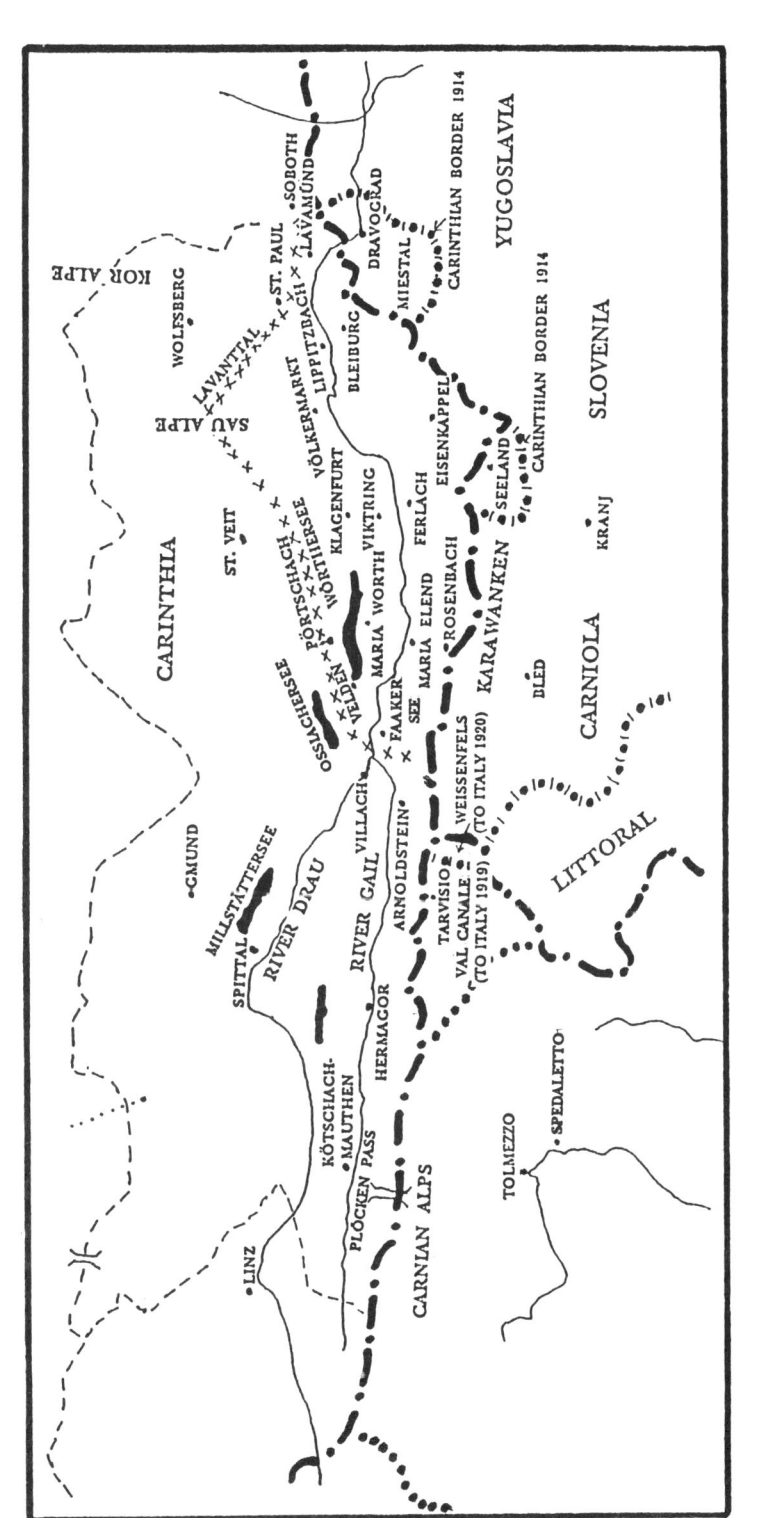

ACKNOWLEDGEMENTS

Some forty years have passed since I was involved in a minor way in the British occupation of Austria. Most of the political and military leaders of the time are no longer with us, but fortunately they have left to us and history a profusion of documentation in the Government files at the Public Record Office. I have accordingly made extensive use of these files in the preparation of this book and I am therefore pleased to make due acknowledgement to the Keeper of the Public Records at Kew. Material from this source is reproduced by permission of the Controller of Her Majesty's Stationery Office.

In addition, I am pleased to acknowledge the help afforded me by the public libraries of Reading, Newport Rhode Island, and New York in tracing historical documents of the period.

I am indebted to the following for their permission to reproduce the illustrations included in this book: The Imperial War Museum; Wilhelm Wadl, Landesarchiv, Klagenfurt; Landesarchiv Graz; Major Lambie; Herbert Fillafer; Österreichisches Institut Für Zeitgeschichte, Wien – Bildarchiv.

I also wish to record my gratitude to the following for their valuable help and encouragement: Dr Wilhelm Wadl, Landesarchiv, Klagenfurt; Dr Augustin Malle, Slovene Institute, Klagenfurt; Dr Dieter Neumann, Villach Museum; the Landesarchiv, Graz; Major Lambie, former SOE officer; Josef Tusch, Technical College, Villach; Aurel Woronka, Gymnasium, Villach; Herbert Fillafer, former Police Official, Villach.

My thanks are also due to the Macmillan Press Ltd for permission to reproduce material from Harold Macmillan's books *Tides of Fortune* and *War Diaries*; to Laurence Pollinger Ltd for permission to draw upon material from Kurt von Schuschnigg's book *Austrian Requiem*; to the BBC for permission to publish extracts from *File on 4*, 20th May 1986, to Times Newspapers Ltd for permission to make reference to various articles on the Austrian Occupation in *The Times*; and to Mirror Group Newspapers for permission to reproduce material from the *Sunday Mirror* of 8th February 1987. I should also like to acknowledge the help given to me by people who I interviewed in Austria and who prefer to remain anonymous.

The manuscript was typed by my daughter Sylvia Currie and Barbara Lancaster and the proofs were read by Jeff Currie.

I would like to acknowledge the help and advice which I received from the management and staff of the Self Publishing Association who guided the production of the book through from start to finish efficiently and expeditiously.

Finally, I give special thanks to my wife who translated relevant German documents and papers and was my interpreter in my discussions in Austria.

Reading
England
May, 1989

INTRODUCTION

In the early hours of the morning of Saturday 12th March, 1938, German troops crossed the Austrian frontier and proclaimed the Anschluss – the union of Austria with Germany. Due to the massive Nazi propaganda during the previous weeks and months, many Austrians were swept along in a tidal wave of emotional acceptance. However, when the Second World War threw them into armed conflict with the rest of Europe their mood changed to one of utter contempt for their Nazi overlords and Austrians were compelled to fight and die for Hitler's Greater German Reich. Moreover, the iron grip of the Gestapo and SS made resistance more difficult and more dangerous than in other Nazi occupied countries.

In spite of this, thousands of patriotic Austrians did resist the German machine and paid the ultimate sacrifice. In the south in the Provinces of Carinthia and Styria the armed resistance of the "Slovene Carinthians", aided by Yugoslav Partisans, kept the German army, Gestapo and SS under constant attack until the end of the war.

Liberation came only after seven years of Nazi tyranny when, in 1945, the four mighty Allied armies of Britain, France, the United States and Russia crossed the Austrian frontier. They found a people on the verge of starvation in a sea of human misery. By previous arrangement between the "Big Three" (Britain, the United States and the Soviet Union), Austria was split into zones of occupation. This geographical pattern was similar to Germany's with Vienna divided like Berlin. As in Germany, Russia administered the eastern part of the country and their zone surrounded Vienna as their eastern zone of Germany still surrounds Berlin.

Whilst hunger was the most urgent problem to be addressed by the Allied Military Governments of all four Powers, there were other demanding problems requiring attention particularly in the British zone of occupation. Hundreds of thousands of people in fleeing from the battle-fronts had gathered in the Province of Carinthia. This mass of humanity consisted of fugitives from every European country and included tens of thousands of German and Austrian troops who had retreated from the advance of the Russians from the east, from the Yugoslavs from the south and from the British advancing through Italy.

Thousands of refugees had fled from the advancing armies and great numbers of anti-Tito forces had been driven over the frontier into Carinthia in the face of Marshal Tito's victorious army. Thousands of Cossacks who had fought for Hitler against Russia had also found sanctuary in Carinthia. The British were confronted with an awesome responsibility for the protection and rehabilitation of this assorted collection estimated at nearly a million people. But they also faced an even more menacing situation which threatened to prolong the war. The threat came not from the enemy but from an ally – Marshal Tito's Yugoslavia – and the dispute, which almost erupted into armed conflict, concerned the "disputed" Carinthian frontier between Yugoslavia and Austria. This frontier had caused a similar conflict after the First World War at the Peace Conference of St Germain but was settled in 1920 in Austria's favour by a plebiscite.

The problem of denazification was common to all four Allied Powers but in the case of Austria was left to the Austrian Government to investigate and mete out punishment or admonish as appropriate. There were some 600,000 Nazi Party members in Austria at the end of the war and the task for the Government was therefore a formidable one. Most of this number however were ordinary innocent citizens who were victims of opportunism or civil or public servants "encouraged" to join the Party by their employers. Of course there were many fanatical Austrian Nazis and the task of bringing them to justice was never quite completed. The Allies occupied Austria for ten years before a Peace Treaty could be agreed. The delay was due mainly to the intransigence of the Russians who were suspected, with good reason, of having designs to partition the country after the methods employed in Germany and its capital Berlin. If the plan had succeeded – and there were occasions when the Western Allies and many Austrians feared that it might – it would have spelled *finis Austriae* with a finality even more emphatic than the Anschluss. That the Russians retreated in 1955 will remain an unsolved mystery until the files of the Kremlin are open for inspection for, with the exception of Afghanistan, Austria is the only country ever surrendered by the Soviets.

After the Allies had left, the Austrian economy improved slowly at first but in later years dramatically. This was due in no small measure to the resourcefulness of her people and to Western aid, during and after the occupation, especially from the United States through the Marshall Plan.

The status of Austria was made clear by the "Big Three" in Moscow in 1943 in the so-called Moscow Declaration:

> *The Governments of the United Kingdom, the Soviet Union and the United States of America are agreed that Austria, the first free country to fall a victim to Hitler's aggression, shall be liberated from German domination.*
>
> *They regard the annexation imposed upon Austria by Germany on March 15th, 1938, as null and void. They consider themselves in no way bound by any changes effected in Austria since that date. They declare that they wish to see reestablished a free and independent Austria, and thereby to open the way for the Austrian people themselves, as well as those neighbouring states which will be faced with similar problems, to find that political and economic security which is the only basis for lasting peace.*
>
> *Austria is reminded however, that she has a responsibility which she cannot evade for participation in the war on the side of Hitlerite Germany, and that in the final settlement account will inevitably be taken of her own contribution to her liberation.*

It is the last paragraph of this Declaration that accounted for the rather anomalous situation prevailing in Austria immediately after the war. While explicitly recognizing Austria as a victim of Hitlerite German aggression, the Allies announced in that paragraph their intention not to let Austria's sovereignty and independence automatically revive upon liberation, but to subject her, by contrast with other victim countries, to a special "final settlement".

Historians will argue that it was the Moscow Declaration which virtually admonished Austria from guilt but it could be contended that it was the Waldheim affair that again drew attention to this unfortunate era of Austrian history after 40 years of silence.

In considering Austria's part in the Second World War it should not be overlooked that to simply exist, Austrians had to survive five radically different conflicting and often dangerous political systems during the first half of this century: the feudalistic Habsburg reign, the Dollfuss and Schuschnigg totalitarian systems, the repressive Nazi regime and finally the Allied military occupation. There was little hope of stemming the Nazi tide in 1938; to do so would have been brave but futile.

According to Schuschnigg, Germany spent millions of dollars to stimulate the idea of an Anschluss and an operations headquarters was established in Vienna. A large Nazi underground was also in evidence and it is believed that the Vienna police had some 700 underground Nazis in its ranks, or about 10 per cent of the force. There were many cases of treason in high places which only came to light later, so good was the secrecy. Schuschnigg maintained that one of the intelligence cells was actually operating within the Chancellery but he was never able to discover it. One of Schuschnigg's private security men who had been his constant companion went over to the Gestapo on the day after the Anschluss and was promoted to a high position.

The failure of the coup d'etat on 25th July, 1934 when the illegal Nazi movement murdered Chancellor Dollfuss in the Chancellery in Vienna brought about a temporary halt to Nazi infiltration. Munich radio actually broadcast the news of Dollfuss's death twenty four hours before he was murdered. But the respite was short lived and Hitler's attitude never changed. He would annex Austria "sooner or later – one way or another."

History may record, however, that the long years of the Allied occupation, although unpopular (what occupation ever is?), stabilised the Country at a critical period and laid the foundation for her independence and prosperity. The British presence held Carinthia for Austria and the Western Allies' determination to maintain their occupation until the Soviet Union agreed a Peace Treaty saved the Country from almost certain partition.

1

ANSCHLUSS – AUSTRIA UNDER THE SWASTIKA

The night sleeper from Vienna pulled into Salzburg in the early morning of 12th February 1938. One of the coaches was discreetly pushed into a siding. In it was the Chancellor of Austria, Dr Kurt von Schuschnigg who was on his way to Berchtesgaden to a secret meeting with Adolf Hitler, Chancellor of Germany.

The Chancellor's party had left Vienna the previous evening dressed for an alpine skiing holiday so as not to attract attention. At 9.30 am a car arrived at the siding to take Schuschnigg to the Berghof, Hitler's Eagle's Nest. At 11am precisely, the Austrian Chancellor was received on the steps of his Alpine retreat by the Führer who was wearing the brown tunic of the Storm Troop uniform, with the swastika armband, and long black trousers. Later Schuschnigg said of the interview that it would forever remain one of the darkest and most fateful days in Austrian history. No political leader had ever been treated with such arrogance and at the end of the war the Gauleiter (Nazi Governor) of Carinthia, Dr Friedrich Rainer, boasted at his interrogation:

> *Schuschnigg was summoned to Berchtesgaden and battered into submission by Hitler – he had no choice, the Führer began shouting at him and told him he was a disgrace to Europe . . . Ribbentrop told him that it was forbidden to smoke in the Führer's presence . . . man was completely broken, he was finished, and agreed to all demands without difficulty.*

Hitler had always been obsessed with an Anschluss (Union) of Germany and Austria although this was strictly forbidden under both the Treaty of St Germain and the Treaty of Versailles. However, his march into the de-militarised Rhineland unopposed only two years previously had given him both inspiration and encouragement for his next objective – Austria. He was determined that the Austrian Chancellor, who he despised, was not going to stand in his way.

The meeting was to seal the fate of Austria. Hitler addressed his guest rudely throughout as "Herr Schuschnigg" instead of giving him his official title of "Herr Bundeskanzler".

In his presentation of Austria's case for peaceful coexistence between their two countries Schuschnigg declared that he had done everything to prove that he and his government intended to follow a friendly policy towards Germany, to which Hitler responded "So you call this a friendly policy. On the contrary you have done everything to avoid a friendly policy . . . The whole history of Austria is just one uninterrupted act of high treason . . . and I can tell you now Herr Schuschnigg that I am absolutely determined to make an end of all this. The German Reich is one of the Great Powers and nobody will raise his voice if it settles its border problems . . . I have a historic mission and this mission I will fulfil because Providence has destined me to do so . . . who is not with me will be crushed . . . I am carried along by the love of my people . . . wherever I go I need the police only to keep the masses back to save them from being trampled, to curb their boundless enthusiasm but not for my protection."

Of the Austrian border defenses, he boasted "I have only to give an order and in one single night all your ridiculous defence mechanisms are blown to bits. You don't believe you can stop me, or even delay me for half an hour do you? Who knows perhaps you will wake up one morning in Vienna to find us there – just like a spring storm. Don't think for one moment that anybody on earth is going to thwart my decisions – Italy? I see eye to eye with Mussolini, the closest ties of friendship bind me to Italy. And England? England will not move one finger for Austria . . . And France? Well, three [sic] years ago we took the Rhineland with a handful of battalions."

And on complaining about the treatment of Nazis in Austria he warned the Chancellor ". . . it is simply an impossible state of affairs when people are thrown into jail in Austria merely because they sing a song that you don't like [the Horst Wessel Lied] or because they salute each other with 'Heil Hitler'. The persecution of National Socialists in Austria must have an end or else I shall put an end to it."

Finally he offered Schuschnigg one more opportunity to come to terms and to meet his demands and raged "Either we find a solution now, or else events will take their course . . . I can only wait until this afternoon . . . I don't believe in bluffing. All my past is proof of that. I have achieved everything that I have set out to do and have thus become perhaps the greatest German of all history . . . I know that one has to take into account certain peculiarities of the Austrians, but that could be easily taken care of."

At one stage the proceedings got so heated that Schuschnigg's Foreign Minister, Guido Schmidt, was heard to remark that it would not surprise him if they were not both arrested. This possibility was nevertheless treated seriously and a military detachment had already been put on the alert in Salzburg.

In the end Schuschnigg, under protest, agreed to sign a ten-point agreement which constituted a blatant intervention in Austrian affairs. One of the requirements imposed on the Austrian Chancellor was to appoint Seyss-Inquart, a fanatical Nazi, to the Ministerial post of public security with full unlimited control of the police force. Within a month he was Schuschnigg's successor and in October the following year was appointed Deputy Governor of Poland. Hitler's admiration of him knew no limits for, in 1940, he was elevated to the post of High Commissioner (Reichskommissar) of the Netherlands, a post he held until the end of the war.

It was there in the Netherlands, that he ordered 5 million Dutch citizens to be sent to Germany for forced labour and 150,000 Jews to concentration camps in Mauthausen, Sobibor, Auschwitz or Belsen where 120,000 of them died or were murdered. Only 8,000 Dutch Jews survived the war. Among his victims was Anne Frank. Deprived of food in the last winter of the war, many Dutch civilians died of starvation. He also drained the Dutch economy of wealth and art treasures which he directed back to Germany.

Seyss-Inquart was a meek looking Nazi with a heart of stone, always well dressed with an aristocratic appearance and impeccable manners, but like many of his Nazi colleagues, he condoned brutality as a means of winning the approval of his Führer. This was the man who Hitler made an Honorary General in the SS and in the last days of the Third Reich was further elevated to Foreign Minister, one of the highest offices in Hitler's Germany. Seyss-Inquart was found guilty of war crimes before the International Military Tribunal at Nürnberg and hanged on the 16th October 1946. The death ovens of Dachau were lit and his body cremated with the rest of ten top Nazis. Other dedicated Nazis in Austria in March 1938 and obsessed with the Anschluss included Kaltenbrunner (head of the Austrian SS and later succeeded Heydrich), Rainer (SS), Globocnig (SS), Keppler (Nazi Commissioner for Austrian Affairs), Huber (Göring's brother-in-law and Minister of the Interior under Seyss-Inquart), Klausner (Chief of the Nazi Party in Austria), Von Papen (German Minister in Vienna) and Glaise-Hortenau (Seyss-Inquart's Vice-Chancellor).

These leading Nazis ensured that the already massive propaganda was increased during the immediate aftermath of the Berchtesgaden meeting and Schuschnigg's dying efforts to launch a plebiscite were doomed. Hitler would have none of it and at dawn on Saturday 12th March, exactly one month to the day after Berchtesgaden he gave his army the order to march and one hundred thousand German troops crossed the Austrian frontier. In the towns and villages from the border to Vienna flags and buntings welcomed the invaders and crowds lined the streets with arms raised in the Nazi salute. Banners, already prepared for the occasion, were strung across the streets carrying messages of encouragement for the Führer:

Wir danken dem Führer (We thank the Führer)*:*
Schluss mit der Knechtschaft (An end to oppression)*:*
Wir grüssen den Führer (We greet the Führer)*:*

On March 15th, 1939, Hitler stood on the balcony of the Hofburg Palace in Vienna to a tumultuous welcome from a quarter of a million delirious Viennese with arms raised in the Nazi salute in the Heldenplatz below. Hitler had taken Austria without a shot being fired in anger but it was the spark that would set Europe ablaze eighteen months later when the whole European continent would become embroiled in the Second World War.

In the evening Hitler arrived in his beloved Linz in triumph and three days later stood on the balcony of the Hofburg Palace in Vienna to a tumultuous welcome from a quarter of a million delirious Viennese, both young and old, with arms raised in the Nazi salute in the Heldenplatz below. Today no one will admit to having been there. It was a day that saw Austria festooned with Nazi flags – red with a black swastika in a white centre circle: The Anschluss was proclaimed and Austria had lost her identity. The name "Austria" was zipped off the map and became known as "Ostmark", a province, or Nazi Gau, of the greater German Reich. Immediately after the declaration all civil and public servants were required to take the Nazi oath and swear allegiance to the regime or be dismissed. Some 70,000 political opponents, Jews and antifascist elements were rounded up and thrown into concentration camps. Thousands more fled to neighbouring countries, and to Britain and America, many to continue the fight against Nazi Germany. In Carinthia, however, many Nazi elements did not even wait for the invasion and SS flags and banners were raised as early as the afternoon of 11th March. Non Austrians (e.g. Jews) were forbidden to wear the swastika and the brutal elimination of the Jews, the "Voldsschädlinge", started in Carinthia and Styria on 16th March and by the 18th they had all but disappeared.

Any Jews who may have survived the Voldsschädlinge would certainly be caught in the Nazi net a few months later in the "Reichskristallnacht" (Reich Crystal Night). This was the infamous night of 9th November when SA gangs were released on Jews and Jewish property throughout the Greater German Reich to smash windows, damage furniture and confiscate Jewish houses and shops.

> *Kristallnacht in Villach still haunts me. I was twelve years of age and was returning home through the town when I was shocked to witness SA gangs smashing windows and tossing furniture on to the street and then setting light to it. As I passed the house of my school chum, whose parents were Jewish, two SA men were trying to force their grand piano through the upstairs window. To do this required heavy hammer blows to knock bits off the piano so that they could throw it out of the window to the street below. As I passed I watched horrified as the piano suddenly plunged to the ground and was pounced upon by jubilant SA thugs and quickly broken up. My chum did not appear in school next day. I never saw her again.*

Throughout the Greater German Reich, Kristallnacht left in its trail one hundred Jews murdered, 26,000 Jews arrested and 200 synagogues burnt or destroyed. Of the 44 synagogues in Nazi-occupied Austria, only one was left intact because Aryan houses might have burned down with it. And the world remained silent. It took Austria many years to commemorate the horrors that befel Austrian Jews in the days following the Anschluss and it was not until 1988 that a monument was unveiled to this effect in the Albertina Platz in Vienna. One of the statues is low to the ground depicting an old Jew on hands and knees scrubbing the pavement with a toothbrush – something Jews had to perform for the amusement of their masters the Viennese Nazis. Others were forced to clean public lavatories and the toilets in the headquarters of the SS or SA.

All Nazi sympathisers who may have supported Schuschnigg were cleansed and reinstated. Photographs of Hitler, framed or unframed, were immediately available for sale in the shops and uniforms were advertised as "tailored to the SS and SA specifications". Music shops in Klagenfurt stocked 6,000 music sheets of the "Horst Wessel Lied" and "Deutschland Uber Alles" and headmasters were instructed, via the newspapers, to order a "suggested" number for use in their schools. Everyone was advised to shop at "your Party comrades". The Neue Platz in Klagenfurt and the Hauptplatz in Villach each took the name "Adolf Hitler Platz"!

The Catholic church in Austria which prior to the Anschluss had possessed almost supreme religious power, was also forced to come to terms with the new regime. Cardinal Innitzer, the Catholic primate of Austria sent personal greetings to the Führer as he was about to enter Vienna on 14th March. He assured him that the swastika would be hoisted on the churches and all over Vienna the church bells would ring a welcome to the leader of all Germans in celebration of the momentous occasion.

Before Hitler flew out of the Capital on the evening of 15th March, the cardinal drove to the Hotel Imperial to pay his respects to the Führer. As he got out of his car he turned to face the large crowd which had gathered and stretched out his arm in the Nazi salute. At his meeting with Hitler in his hotel suite he promised that the church would cooperate with the new State – "We all have the same German blood in our veins" he said, and Hitler was delighted.

Graz, Opernring, April 20th, 1938, a group of top Nazis await the arrival of General von Bock who later commanded German Army Group Centre for the attack on Moscow with 51 divisions.

Hitler Youth parade in Graz (Opernring) to celebrate the Anschluss in 1938.

On 18th March Innitzer wrote to the newly appointed Gauleiter Bürkel of Vienna assuring him that there would be no conflict between church and state and all Austrian Catholics would have his personal blessing to vote "yes" in Hitler's impending plebiscite arranged for 10th April. He finished the letter with the greeting "Heil Hitler". All this was too much for the Vatican and Pope Pius XI summoned Innitzer to Rome to explain his actions. Meantime Hitler duly claimed his famous majority on 10th April, when over 99 per cent of Austrians voted "yes" for the Anschluss. The figures showed that approximately 4,453,000 of the 4,484,000 electorate had voted "yes", only 11,924 had dared to vote "no" and 5,776 had the courage to spoil their papers. Innitzer got no thanks from his Nazi friends however, who accused him now of divided loyalties. On 8th October a Nazi mob consisting mainly of youths stormed the Cardinal's palace and did considerable damage to the interior. At a rally on the Heldenplatz five days later, Gauleiter Bürkel addressed the crowd and made a brutal attack on the church and demonstrators displayed their banners proclaiming "Innitzer and the Jews are one breed", "priests to the gallows" and "Innitzer to Dachau", "Without the Jews and without Rome we shall build a true German Cathedral". The church in Austria virtually disappeared underground for the next seven years of the Nazi occupation

The Nazi leaders were jubilant, especially Göring and Ribbentrop who, on the 11th March had been dining at 10 Downing Street and on the day after the invasion the following telephone conversation took place:

Göring from Berlin to Ribbentrop in London, 13th March, 1938, 9.15 am.

Göring: *You know already that the Führer has charged me with the running of the Government, and I thought I would ring you and give all the necessary information. The jubilation in Austria is indescribable – you can hear that on the radio.*

Ribbentrop: *Yes, it is fantastic, isn't it?*

Göring: *Yes, indeed. Our last march – the re-occupation of the Rhineland – is completely eclipsed by this event, especially as far as the*

> *joy of the people is concerned . . . The Führer was deeply moved when I talked to him last night. You must realise that it is the first time he has seen his home again . . .*

Ribbentrop: *My conferences here in London are at an end. If I hang around here with no good reason it might look funny. I received the very best impression of Chamberlain, by the way . . .*

Göring: *Well, then, I shall see you here. I am very much looking forward to seeing you. The weather here in Berlin is wonderful. I am sitting here wrapped up in blankets on my terrace in the bracing air and drinking my coffee. Later I have to go in and deliver my speech. The birds are singing, and every now and then I can hear through the radio the outburst of joy and jubilation over there. It is collosal.*

Ribbentrop: *Oh. it is wonderful!*

The heady days of the Anschluss lasted just 18 months more when Austria was dragged into the Second World War, a war in which she would lose 350,000 of her manhood, killed in action fighting for the Nazi cause. Moreover, she would be occupied by foreign armies for nearly eighteen years.

Schuschnigg was arrested and spent the next seven years in the concentration camps of Sachsenhausen, Flossenburg and Dachau where he found himself on Himmler's death list. He survived, however, and was freed by the Americans, who on 4th May 1945 sent him to Capri to convalesce after his ordeal. On being interviewed there he said that he thought the best thing possible for Austria now was a long period of Allied Government. He mentioned that one of the crimes the Gestapo accused him of was engineering a Habsburg coup d'etat with the British in 1934. They were convinced that he was in a plot of this kind. He showed pride at the measure of Hitler's hate of him. "He hated me like the plague" he remarked "as he couldn't bear people standing up to him. That's why he wanted me to disappear." He said that there was no truth in the story that he was made to listen to records of Hitler's speeches in the early years of his imprisonment. And there was no truth either in the arc lamp story, namely that he was exposed day and night to bright lights placed in his cell. He was convinced that if the plebiscite of 13th March 1938 had been held his Government would have secured 75% – 80% of the votes.

After the war Schuschnigg moved to the United States and took up a Professorship in the University of St Louis where he remained until his retirement in 1967 when he returned to Austria. He died in 1977 aged 80.

In considering Austria's involvement in the Anschluss, however, as we shall see later, the seeds were sown as long ago as 1919 at the Paris Peace Conference after the Treaty of St Germain had decimated the Austro-Hungarian Empire. Unofficial plebiscites in Tirol and Salzburg gave massive majorities for union with the German State of Bavaria and confirmed the prevalent feeling in Austria in the nineteen twenties.

Hitler, aided by his bully boys simply bided his time and struck at the opportune moment. Indeed he had promised in 1925 in Mein Kamf ("My crusade") that "Germanism could be safeguarded only by the destruction of Austria". The plans for invasion were completed by the Autumn of 1937 and when the Duke and Duchess of Windsor visited Göring in his palatial country home, Karinhall, the Duchess noticed a large wall map which treated Austria as part of Germany. She asked the Duke to query Göring on the matter which he did and Göring responded with a grin that it was a new map and since it was certain that Austria would soon want to be part of Greater Germany it saved him the bother of having a new map made when it happened. And later on 5th November at a conference he held with his senior political and military advisers, Hitler officially announced his intention to annex Austria. A copy of the minutes of this meeting is held in the Cabinet War Rooms.

Even the most fervent Austrian Nazis, however, would probably have avoided the Anschluss like the plague if they had known of the dire consequencies to come. At the peak of the Nazi period in Austria there were about 600,000 Nazi Party members. With a population of six and a half million this number formed only a minority, albeit a vociferous and important one. Even allowing for the families of these party members that some historians like to include, the total was still only about one quarter of the population. Schuschnigg, in his proposed plebiscite for the Austrian people for Sunday 13th March was asking "Are you in favour of a *free* and German, an *independent* and social, a Christian and *United* Austria?" It was estimated by observers at the time that, from an electorate of about 4½ million people, Schuschnigg could rely on the support of 3 million workers and peasant farmers and half a million Jewish supporters. With sympathetic Monarchist and Fatherland Front votes added to that number Schuschnigg's own forecast of gaining a 75%/80% majority against the Anschluss was probably, if anything, conservative. Little wonder that Hitler flew into a rage when he was told of the proposed plebiscite and closed the German-Austrian border at Salzburg on the morning of 11th March at 4.30 am. German divisions stationed at Munich had already been mobilised — destination Austria.

However, in spite of Schuschnigg's confidence of a victory at the polls, there was considerable support for the Anschluss at all levels of Austrian society. Even Karl Renner, Chancellor twice immediately after both World Wars, supported a pro-Anschluss policy for 20 years from 1918 until 1938. After the war on being asked to comment on the reason why Austria offered no resistance to the German army in 1938 Renner reasoned that this was to a large extent because Hitler could not deprive the Austrian workers of any liberties. Dollfuss he maintained had already taken them away and Hitler at least promised them work and bread. However he agreed that the Anschluss idea was now dead and inspired nothing but disgust. "The Hitler regime had in seven years abolished the independent Republic of Austria and wiped out the name of Austria."

2

FROM THE DESERT TO THE ALPS

In the early afternoon of 7th May 1945, Lieutenant Edwards and Sergeant Altonburrow negotiated the steep winding alpine road over the Plöcken Pass and drove into Austria. They arrived in the little village of Kötschach-Mauthen to the relief and jubilation of the inhabitants and were greeted with garlands of flowers. They were the first British troops in Austria.

The first Britsh troops to enter Austria in the late afternoon of 7th May to the jubilation of the people of Kötschach - Mauthen who welcomed them with garlands of flowers.

Edwards and Altonburrow headed one of two spearheads of the Eighth Army, 41 Tank Squadron of the Battle Axe Division of 5 Corps advancing on Austria. The other was moving forward across the Isonzo river from Trieste towards Val Canale. The Battle Axe

Division had met little or no resistance in their dash from Tolmezzo, but at a Gasthaus on the pass they found food still warm which the Germans had no time to enjoy. They had left in a hurry as they had done from the surrounding farms and villages. A ragged crowd of prisoners had drifted towards the advancing British, their main desire to escape from the Italian and Yugoslav partisans. The Germans retreating with all haste from Italy were being followed by a disorderly rabble of non-German satellite troops described by the Austrian and Italian peasants as little more than bandits and who the Germans had left to their own resources. A pitched battle broke out near Mauthen between German troops and Cossacks who in despair had turned against their German ally. Since 3rd May some 10,000 Cossack troops had been retreating from Tolmezzo over the Plöcken Pass, plundering and skirmishing with straggling Wehrmacht units. The local German garrison requested permission to join the British troops in an effort to subdue the Russians.

In the evening the forward troops of the Battle Axe Division pushed on to Lienz.

The first British soldier to arrive in Klagenfurt on 8th May 1945 is greeted in the Heiligengeistplatz by the provisional Landeshauptmann (Governor Stephan Tauschitz and Landesrat (County Councillor) Hans Herke.

The second prong of the British attack was aimed at Klagenfurt, the Provincial Capital of Carinthia. The Isonzo Valley had experienced heavy fighting during the First World War and the many Italian war cemeteries in the area could bear witness to this. It was also the setting for Ernest Hemingway's "A Farewell to Arms" whose hero, Lieutenant Frederic Henry, was a young American attached to an Italian ambulance unit on the Isonzo front. The enemy were the Austrians. British intelligence had confirmed that Tito too was advancing on Austria and Klagenfurt was also the objective. If the Trieste situation was not to be repeated, where Tito had arrived only a day before the British and claimed the City for Yugoslavia, Alexander's Eighth Army would have to move fast.

The task was given on 2nd May to 27 Lancers with 2 Rifle Brigade mopping up in the rear. Next morning, however, the Lancers were held up by an SS Unit around Ospedaletto which refused to surrender and commenced shelling. The advance units nearly clashed with Tito's forces on the Isonzo who were claiming the territory for Yugoslavia. In addition to mopping up the remaining German forces the British were now mixed up in a political quarrel with their ally.

Commendable restraint and diplomacy were exhibited by all ranks under trying conditions of a nature completely foreign to their experience. This set of circumstances held up the British advance some days but intelligence received on 7th May suggested that the Germans were retreating. The Rifle Brigade thereupon pushed on to take Tarvisio, and 27 Lancers reached the Austrian border without further opposition although encountering numerous enemy troops. A parley took place between Major General Murray and SS Major General Harmel in Tarvisio which was occupied by both British and German troops. The British advance was further delayed, however, by the Germans demolishing the road and rail bridges.

At dawn on 8th May units of the 27 Lancers, First Derby Yeomanry and First Guards Brigade crossed the Austrian frontier and raced for Klagenfurt. Third Grenadier Guards and Third Welsh Guards occupied Villach.

At 9.30 in the morning the first British troops, from the Rifle Brigade, entered Klagenfurt and occupied the town. Although they had met "considerable Tito irregular forces already in the area", the British had won the race for Klagenfurt, but only by a few hours. This "possession" was important in the days and months ahead when Tito's territorial claims on Carinthia came under discussion by the Allies.

The British advance units in Klagenfurt were met by Stefan Tauschitz, deputy Landeshauptmann (Deputy Governor) in the Villacher Strasse. In the Heiligengeist Platz they were welcomed on behalf of the "Carinthian Provisional Government" and were led to the Landhaus to receive a greeting on behalf of the people of Carinthia.

British troops arrive in Klagenfurt on 8th May 1945, their tanks decorated in flowers.

To their surprise the British were received by a Carinthian Provisional Government (Landesregierung) which had been hastily set up during the last week of the war. They were also informed that a Provisional National Government (Bundesregierung) had been formed by the Russians in Vienna under Dr Karl Renner.

The Landersregierung had been formed in spite of the fact that no organised Austrian movement was allowed to exist in the Country. Certain groups and individuals of the pre-Anschluss parties, however, had made preparation for the time when Nazi Germany would be defeated and the repressive Nazi regime destroyed. It is likely that they were known to the very efficient but ruthless Gestapo control system and allowed to continue as constituting no serious danger to the régime. The Nazi Gauleiter Rainer, however, was determined to govern Carinthia to the very end and to ensure that the retreat routes for the German armies in Yugoslavia were kept open and that General Löhr's surrender should be made to the British and not to Tito.

AUSTRIA : ZONES OF OCCUPATION

Now that Hitler was dead, Rainer considered himself bound by his allegiance to Dönitz and was prepared to make Carinthia a battleground if necessary. He was only prepared to resign if the British troops were actually marching in, but in radio broadcasts during the last few days of the war he called upon Carinthian citizens, and the SS, to make a last ditch stand against the British. However the efforts of a few Carinthian patriots forced Rainer to flee before the British entered Austria and it was this small group of politicians who formed the Landesregierung, and appointed a Landeshauptman (Governor) as its head.

The personalities concerned were chiefly pre-Anschluss officials. Both the old and the new Governments found themselves faced with a dual problem, surrender to the British and the prevention of invasion by Tito forces. Even the Communist members initially supported a resolution in favour of the territorial integrity of Carinthia. As late as 6th May the Provisional Landesregierung, prepared a surrender mission to the Allied forces in Italy. However owing to the refusal of cooperation by the SS troops in the Val Canale, the impossibility of passing through Tito territory and the report of Italian partisan control in Carnia, on the Austro-Italian border, this mission was constrained to secure indirect contact via the American commander in Salzburg, whence a message was transmitted to Allied Forces Headquarters, Caserta. By the time the mission returned to Klagenfurt, 5 Corps troops had already crossed the frontier.

At mid-day advance units of Tito's Yugoslav Army started arriving at Klagenfurt. Their commander telephoned the Governor, declared themselves as liberators and demanded an official reception. The main army, he said, would arrive at 3 pm. The Governor however had the courage (and the backing of the British) to refuse and informed the commander that the British were already in Klagenfurt and had taken over the town and the Province. When the main units of the Yugoslav Army arrived in the afternoon they met the British face to face in the Bahnhofstrasse. British tolerance and diplomacy were stretched to the limit but fortunately no fighting broke out. In the days and weeks which followed, the patience of the British troops was severely tested as the Yugoslavs deployed their forces in Klagenfurt and the surrounding area.

As evening fell on Carinthia on VE Day, 8th May, Londoners were making whoopee in Trafalgar Square, Parisians were parading arm in arm down the Champs Elysées and New Yorkers were dancing in

Times Square, but there were no celebrations in the British Zone of Austria, for Carinthia was in turmoil.

Yugoslav troops march on Klagenfurt 8th May 1945.

Next morning the Yugoslav troops were entrenched in Klagenfurt and their commander, in ordering the withdrawal of all flags and banners, proceeded to requisition public buildings not already occupied by the British. The Yugoslav Government thereupon declared the Anschluss of Carinthia into Greater Yugoslavia and posters to this effect were erected throughout the Province.

At eight o'clock in the evening the British made contact with Marshal Tolbukhin's Russian Army at Voitsberg, near Graz in Styria. The Russians had come all the way from Stalingrad, the British three thousand miles from the desert. The troops of both sides had a friendly greeting for each other and although the Russians had occupied Styria instead of, as agreed, the British, the meeting was an historic one as well as cordial. For the Eighth Army it was the end of the line. Their task had been accomplished and in a few months they would be disbanded. They would always be regarded as one of the greatest fighting outfits in British military history. Moreover they had the honour of being the first Allied force to land and remain on the European mainland. Their victory in the desert at El Alamein in 1942, coupled with the Russian victory at Stalingrad, is still considered the turning point of the war.

Field Marshal Alexander, Allied Supreme Commander Mediterranean sent a personal message to his troops on the occasion of their victory in Italy:

> *No praise is high enough for your magnificent triumph; my gratitude to you and my admiration is unbounded and only equalled by the pride which is mine of being your Commander in Chief.*

The British Troops in Austria (BTA), however, continued to wear the Eighth Army Crusader shoulder patch with its yellow cross, as a mark of respect, and the BTA transit camp in Villach would take the name "Alamein" and serve the British Zone.

Alamein British Army Camp, Villach.

The British were the last of the Allies to complete the liberation of Austria. The troops of the Soviet Union crossed the Hungarian-Austrian frontier on 29th March although fighting continued in Styria until 9th May. The US 10th Armoured Division reached the River Lech on 28th April when elements crossed the border near Fussen and Vils. French troops entered Vorarlberg on the same day after heavy fighting for the town of Bregenz. Innsbruck was captured on 4th May by the 103 Division and after a 25 mile dash by cavalry units to Salzburg, the City surrendered to the US 7th Army without a fight. On the same day the 7th Army met troops of the US 5th Army from Italy on the Brenner Pass.

On the Italian - Austrian border at Thörl Maglern, the 6th British Armoured Division enter Austria on 9th May 1945.

Austria for the purposes of military occupation was divided into four zones based on her 1937 frontiers as agreed by the Three Powers at the Yalta conference. The Soviet Zone consisted of the Province of Lower Austria and that part of the Province of Upper Austria situated on the left (north) bank of the Danube and the Province of Burgenland. The United States Zone consisted of the Province of Salzburg and that part of the Province of Upper Austria situated on the right (south) bank of the Danube. The French Zone consisted of the Provinces of Tirol and Vorarlberg. The British Zone consisted of the Provinces of Carinthia (including Ost-Tirol) and Styria. The United States had assumed that they would occupy the whole of the Province of Upper Austria but the

Soviet Union's interpretation of the Yalta Agreement split the Province into that portion north of the Danube (Soviet Union) and the portion south of the river (United States). Rather than cause undue conflict at an early stage of the occupation the United States gave way. At Churchill's suggestion, France was invited to participate in the occupation zones, which she agreed to do.

The British Military Government arrived in Klagenfurt on 12th May and immediately held a meeting with the Carinthian Provisional Government and the Yugoslav Commander. It was made clear to both that the British had "entered" Carinthia as victors as Austria had willingly or unwillingly become part of Hitler's war. Consequently the British initially refused to recognise the Provisional Government and it was not until July that a more representative Government was acknowledged by the British Military Government. However it was the Yugoslav presence in Carinthia that dominated British military and political policy in the first months of the occupation.

The Yugoslav Government maintained that its Partisan units, with the help of the 4th Yugoslav Army, had liberated areas of the Province before the arrival of the British. The areas mentioned were "the main regions south of the Drava (Drau), the whole area of Volkermarkt, Klagenfurt itself and Gospa Sveta (Maria Saal), historic centre of the Slovene people." The statement was clearly an exaggeration in order to make a political point, though it is true that pockets of Partisans were already in Carinthia before the British, and 5 Corps reports confirm this to be the case. It is evident too that some skirmishing took place between the Wehrmacht troops and the Partisans before the British arrived.

There were many other problems for the British, however, which required urgent attention. Much of the civilian population was on the point of starvation. The Germans had denuded the Province of farm produce over the last year of the war to feed their own people. Food supply had therefore become a priority and the British had to make arrangements to have enough supplies brought in to see the population through the immediate crisis. Throughout the summer they would ensure that the farmers were made aware of the situation, although food supplies would still require to be imported to see the people through the coming winter. The situation was exasperated by the thousands of Yugoslav troops who relied on food supplies solely through confiscation.

In addition, thousands of troops of all nations were converging on

Carinthia to surrender, and when the first British units entered Volkermarkt on 9th May they met an unbelievable number of troops from a variety of countries who were still involved in fighting. Germans, Croats and Hungarians were withdrawing into Styria in the face of the Russian advance to surrender. Yugoslavs and Bulgarians were trying to prevent them, and Russians and Bulgarians entered Dravograd (Unterdrauburg) where skirmishing took place with thousands of Chetniks (Royalists) fleeing from Yugoslavia towards the British lines. Thousands of Displaced Persons (DPs) began arriving from Yugoslavia and from many eastern countries. Several hundred thousand troops from different countries had arrived by the middle of May and had to be thrown together into huge camps awaiting repatriation.

The British did their best to defuse the situation with as much tact and diplomacy as they could muster. Clashes between the various factions, however, were unavoidable and skirmishes erupted from time to time and hundreds were killed. In Rosental, partisans and SS White Guards fought several engagements around Ferlach and the occupancy of the town changed several times.

Due to the breakdown on all fronts, Carinthia had thus become a huge gathering ground and by the end of May nearly one million fugitives had arrived in the Province from over 30 nationalities. Thousands of refugees were fleeing from the Russians and from Yugoslavia in never ending columns and some half a million German troops from two army groups (E and C) were retreating from three fronts. Thousands from satellite states, Croats, Hungarians, Rumanians and Bulgarians etc. were streaming into the Drau Valley. The Croats included Domobranci (Croat Defence force), Ustasi (extreme Croat Nationalists) and the Bela Garda (White Guards – Slovene Military force). In addition there were some 40,000 Cossacks, 54,000 Displaced Persons, 20,000 British, French and Italian prisoners of war, who had been liberated from Stalags and Oflags XVIII at Lienz, Spittal, Villach and Wolfsberg, and even 2,000 German citizens working for the Nazi régime in Carinthia.

Entries from 5 Corps daily reports (6th Armoured Division) testify to the appalling conditions prevailing in Carinthia in May.

13th Surrendered personnel:

    St Veit   30,000

Feldkirch	10,000
Viktring	8,000
Many SS and police	
Cossacks	4,500
Ukrainians not estimated	
Croats	10,000
Total	85,000 in Division Zone

But many other types mainly mercenaries and from General Löhr's Army Group E expected back over border after surrendering to Tito.

Yugoslav infiltration increasing in quantity.

Looting by Yugoslavs.

Warnings from Yugoslavs that British troops would be expelled from Carinthia.

16th   Anti-British and American Yugoslav rally in Klagenfurt.

20th   5 Corps decided on detailed action to be taken should it become necessary to eliminate Yugoslav forces in 5 Corps area.

But at 00.01 hours Yugoslav forces decided to withdraw.

09.30 750 Croats handed over.

21.00 more Croats handed over.

First Guards Battalion resumed responsibility for Velden area.

23rd   3,000 Croats evacuated to Yugoslavia.

24th	450 Croats evacuated to Yugoslavia.
	1,000 Serbs handed over to Yugoslavia.
27th	Disarming Cossacks.
29th	Disposal of Cossack officers completed.
30th	4,000 Cossacks, other ranks, handed over to Soviets.
	4,950 Slovenes handed over to Yugoslavs.
	50 Croats handed over to Yugoslavia.

The 5 Corps report for May 1945 concludes:

1. The infantry with their support troops acting on difficult orders, or sometimes no orders at all, handling all relations with Tito's forces tactfully and sensibly. In the face of irritating provocation they continued to act with such restraint that not a single unfortunate incident was reported.

2. The concentration of many thousands of enemy personnel had been effected in spite of chaotic road conditions, the bewildering miscellany of almost every European and Western Asiatic race or tribe, sometimes in Wehrmacht uniform, but more often in small national groups of their own, and the refusal of various groups of Yugoslav partisans to regard the armistice as binding for many days after its declaration.

In order to establish control over this precarious situation, the British Military Government invoked a curfew from 8.30 pm until 6 am. In June this period was reduced to 10 pm until 5 am, in August from 11 pm until 4 am and was not lifted completely until October.

Travel by civilians was restricted first to 10 km and raised to 20 km in June. Residence permits were introduced and, in October, identity cards, which remained until the end of the occupation.

On arrival in Klagenfurt at the beginning of June, the censorship organisation found that civilian post had been stopped and mail was lying in sealed post-boxes and offices throughout Carinthia. On the other hand civilian telephones were in operation provided both parties to a call were on the same exchange, whilst a limited number of callers had permission to make calls from one exchange to another. The monitoring of telephone calls was a first priority of the censorship organisation, and, second the examination of impounded mail of which there were 200,000 items. Long distance telephone calls were forbidden and internal mail, which was the only mail permissible, was restricted to non-illustrated post cards and 20 gramme letters, and was censored.

The Western Allies in Austria were normally required to follow Military Government procedures adopted in Germany. For example, Eisenhower's statement on 14th May:

> *My attention has been called to press reports of instances of senior US officers treating Nazi and high German officers as a friendly enemy. Any such instance has been in direct violation of my express and long standing orders. Drastic measures have been set in motion to assume the termination of these errors forthwith . . . individuals concerned . . . will be personally acquainted with the expression of my definite disapproval.*

Similarly, a civilian fraternisation ban in Germany was also adopted in Austria. The ban was a difficult one to enforce, especially in Carinthia due to special political circumstances prevailing, but it was observed by the vast majority of the troops in the spirit of discipline and loyalty. The ban, for example, could not be applied to children, and boys were in the habit of swarming over British vehicles of all types. At the direction, therefore, of General Eisenhower and Field Marshal Montgomery, the ban was modified, and from July conversation was permitted with adults in public places. Troops were still forbidden to enter Austrian homes, but because of the rapid progress being made in carrying out de-nazification policies in removing prominent Nazis from positions of responsibility, the fraternisation ban in Austria was removed in September.

Another problem which the British faced in those early days was the Russian occupation of Styria. Information on what was happening in that region was difficult to obtain but in a minute to the Prime Minister dated 12th July, Anthony Eden stated that he had learned from "a good many sources that the Russians have been deporting ablebodied Austrians to the Soviet Union." These were believed to consist mainly of Austrians against whom there was a charge of active support and sympathy for the Nazis "though Russian methods for deciding on such matters are extremely rough and ready." Eden continued, "There is no doubt at all that the Russians have been carrying out wholesale removals of industrial equipment from both Lower Austria and Styria." It was also reported to the Foreign Office that "personal property was limited to one of everything – knife, spoon, chair, etc. and that all surplus was being moved to Russia." Eden concluded by reminding Churchill that the British position on those matters was made quite clear to the Russians in a note addressed to the Soviet Government in April based on a proposed telegram to Stalin which Churchill had been concerting with President Roosevelt just before his death and which contained the following passage:

> *His Majesty's Government are sure that the Soviet Government will agree that our common purpose might well be prejudiced by unilateral action on the part of any one of the occupying powers in regard to the removal of industrial plant and equipment, regardless of whether or not this was German owned, or the elimination, without regard to their attitude towards the Nazis, of Austrians who might prove useful in re-establishing the Austrian administration and economy.*

The British could do little more to alleviate the situation until they moved into Styria, which they eventually did on 24th July when British troops entered Graz to an enthusiastic welcome. General Weir addressed the Citizens from the Rathaus (Town Hall). On the previous evening an advance party of the 70th Field Regiment Royal Artillery had been lavishly entertained by the Russians before taking over from them.

The British discovered that all transport in Graz, including bicycles, had been requisitioned by the Russians and only seven lorries were left for civilians. By cunning means, however, until the British arrived, the Austrians tried to stem the tide of confiscation and deportation by hiding specialised machinery and sending most of the employees on indefinite leave.

The troops of the British 46th Division entered Graz on 24th July 1945 after the evacuation of Soviet occupying forces. The photograph shows their General Weir standing on a armoured car addressing the people in the main square of the city.

In Styria the Russians had already set up a Provisional Government, and the British confirmed the appointment of Reinhard Machold as Landeshauptmann. Most of the other members of the Government were retained. Machold said in a speech on Radio Graz on 9th August:

> *On 23rd July Soviet troops in Graz and other parts of Styria were replaced by British troops and the Commander of the British occupation troops entrusted me with the formation of the new Government.*

During the three months of office behind me, I have been and still am weighed down by many anxieties, the gravest being how to feed our people . . . Let the peasant on the land never forget that the toil of his hands is needed to produce food for the Styrian population. Many people do not seem to realise yet the seriousness of the situation. There is a shortage of manual labour, and in many cases the labour is actually available but is apparently unwilling to work. I appeal to everyone not to evade rendering the necessary service to work.

Just as in other Provinces of Austria, democratically elected Provincial Governments were formed in Carinthia and Styria on 25th November. The long transition to Democracy had begun.

Friedrich Rainer, Nazi Gauleiter for Carinthia was arrested by the British and, after testifying at the Nürnberg war trials, was handed over to Tito to be tried for war crimes. He was found guilty and hanged.

At his interrogation on 8th July Rainer said:

History will prove that it wasn't Seyss or Klausner but Clobocnig and me who were responsible for the events of those days [run-up to the Anschluss]. Seyss always had a bad conscience and [after the Anschluss] told me I would become his adviser. Seyss tried to get certain documents that I was holding and two years ago he wrote to me for them for a short history which he was writing but I wouldn't let him have them. The thing he did publish in the end was superficial nonsense.

I never put anything down in writing about these events, a very good thing really now that things have come to this. If I compare the days of 9th-11th March 1938 with those of 7th May [1945] onwards, I must say that the latter – the days of the counter putsch, were far more unhappy!

In the first I kept the initiative to the end. And the end was certainly happier – by God so much happier.

Now I only want to see how best I can straighten out my

private life. A beautiful German tragedy; Faust Part 2, Heaven and Hell at the beginning and the end – one's own little piece of ground, one's house and garden.

Rainer maintained that the only appreciation he ever got from Hitler was his announcement, after the Anschluss, that all of them involved – Keppler, Kaltenbrunner, Klausner and Rainer etc. – would be accepted into the SS.

Hitler's Austrian Gauleiters on parade just after the Anschluss in 1938. Seyss-Inquart can be seen on the extreme left and Rainer, Gauleiter of Carinthia and Überreither Gauleiter of Styria are second and fourth from the right respectively. The Gauleiter (leiter = leader) in Austria was the Governor of the Province and had a direct line of communication to the Führer. Below him came the Stellvertreter (Deputy) Gauleiter, Kreisleiter, the Ortsgruppenleiter, the Zellenleiter and finally the Blockleiter. The organisation was a strict system of order and obedience.

The Nazi Gauleiter of Styria, Siegfried Überreither, was also arrested by the British, but escaped before he could be tried for war crimes and fled to Argentina where he lived comfortably until his death 30 years later.

Odilo Globocnig became head of "Action Reinaard" in Lublin and was the overseer for the extermination camps of Treblinka, Sobibor and Belzec.

He was once sent for by the Commandant of Treblinka, Eberl, who was having problems "processing" the victims through the camp and handling the mountains of corpses. When Globocnig arrived at the gates of Treblinka on a hot day in August 1943 he preferred not to inspect the camp because of the stench of rotting flesh which penetrated the air. Instead he stopped at Eberl's office and demanded to know why he was accepting so many prisoners when he could only process 3,000 per day through the gas ovens. Eberl was promptly sacked and Globocnig appointed a more determined Commandant in Wirth who proceeded to improve the efficiency of the operation.

If the troops' task as an army of occupation was not always light, it was by the end of July at least peaceful and friendly. Life on the shores of the beautiful Wörthersee between Villach and Klagenfurt was most pleasant. The warm Carinthian summer was a welcome tonic that allowed the troops to relax and enjoy as much leisure time as possible. Along the shore of the lake almost every hotel and villa and their grounds became a rest centre for the pleasure of bathing, boating or fishing, Velden and Pörtschach being the most popular centres. In Villach the British requisitioned the magnificent Park Hotel for NCOs and other ranks while the historical Post Hotel became the Officers' rest centre.

British Military Police on patrol on the Wörthersee.

Similar facilities were requisitioned in Klagenfurt and other resorts where battle-weary troops were able to relax. These centres would continue to be available to British forces posted to British Troops in Austria (BTA) until a Peace Treaty was agreed.

Meantime in Vienna Karl Renner's Provisional Government, supported entirely by the Soviet Union, set out to gain the support of the

Western Powers.

Renner's account of how he came to form the Provisional Government of Austria in 1945 is the stuff of stories. Yet by all accounts his story is true and he became the Chancellor of Austria for a second time. The first time, ironically enough, was at the end of the First World War in 1918.

Dr Karl Renner, at the age of 75 with his sister Poldi - Deutsch - Renner in the grounds of his house at Gloggnitz. (8th August 1945).

Renner's story is that on Easter Sunday, the 10th April, Russian troops occupied Gloggnitz about 50 miles south west of Vienna where Renner lived. Early in the morning Nazi political emissaries had informed the inhabitants that two trains were ready at the station for those who wished to leave. Renner decided to remain behind. After the trains had departed with the Germans, the Russians occupied the town without opposition and no casualties. Later the Russians carried out a door to door, room to room search for concealed German soldiers and weapons and what took place during these searches "people of Gloggnitz are not likely to forget". He had to remain in his house, like his neighbours, until Tuesday morning when he made up his mind to seek out the Russian commanding officer so that he might be able to obtain "protection for the people". The streets were empty except for a few Russian troops "here and there to which I tried in vain to speak".

Renner had no Russian and the troops had no German but eventually he was taken to Soviet headquarters in a quiet side street. The officer in charge arranged for him to be sent to the village of Köttlach where several Russian officers knew his name.

There he explained that the majority of Austrian's had, in view of Hitler's initial successes and his promises, assumed a hopeful attitude. After his methods of depression and warlike aims, however, they took a dislike to the Anschluss and had longed for the re-establishment of an independent Austria. The Russians apparently put forward the argument that Austrians had been fighting on all battlefields and some had been prominent Nazis, to which Renner replied that the overwhelming power of the Nazis' propaganda and their brutal methods were the only reason.

Renner explained to the Russians why he was still alive. From the first days of the war it became certain to him where Hitler's venture would lead. He had reckoned for some years that Austria might some day again want his experience which he had acquired as Chancellor in the years 1918 to 1920 and his reputation as Chairman of the Austrian delegation at the negotiations of the Treaty of St Germain. He had therefore done all he could not to attract Nazi persecution. However, he said, with all his good intentions he was as helpless as the people of Austria as a whole with no means of action, no press and "not even one typewriter".

The Russians thereupon agreed to help him and asked if he was ready to fulfil his long cherished plans. After much reflection he agreed to take the risk of "jeopardising my reputation and that of the Party and my existence as a politician in the hope of enabling Austria to free herself of the chains binding her to Germany."

Two days later he was taken to meet "an astonishing number of senior officers" and agreed to issue several proclamations to the Austrian people, appealing to them to proclaim their independence of the German Reich and to return to the democratic constitution of the Republic giving him a mandate as the last freely elected President of the Austrian Parliament.

Karl Renner arrived in Vienna on 21st April, and six days later established "a central Government for the whole country" with him as Chancellor. Renner was surprised, perhaps naively, to find that the British and Americans could not accept his Government. They were suspicious of the Communist influence for one thing and, for another, it had not been formed from free elections. They had good reason to be suspicious because the Government included three Communist members who had spent the last ten years in Moscow and re-entered Austria under Russian auspices. Of the 21 Under Secretaries of State, seven were Communists and occupied key positions.

The British considered Renner a typical moderate politician of the opportunist type who owed a good deal of his popularity to his obvious good nature and typical Viennese charm and temperament. He was a man of learning and culture but they considered him possibly too old at 75 to lead the Austrian Government at a crucial period in its history. The British had not yet entered Austria and the Americans were just crossing the border into Tirol. Moreover the British were suspicious that the Russians had their eye on Renner for some time past as a possible candidate for a "free" Austrian Government. As far as the British and Americans were concerned the Government could only be considered as a Provisional Government with authority in Vienna only. British policy was to secure the restoration of a free and independent Austrian State and to ensure a representative Government for the whole of Austria as soon as possible.

There is evidence to support the Foreign Office suspicion that Renner could have been a Russian puppet to gradually nudge Austria into the Eastern Block (or at least partition it). The evidence is to be found in the Karl Renner Museum in Gloggnitz. In the last days of March 1945, Stalin gave orders to find out what became of Dr Renner. Renner was therefore known to the Russian Commander at Hochwolkersdorf where he was taken by the Russians after his interrogation in Köttlach. The Commander informed Moscow that he had found Renner whereupon Stalin sent a telegram to the Commander of the Third Ukrainian Front containing the following three points:

> 1. Renner is to be given every support and has to be trusted completely.
>
> 2. Renner should be told that the Commander of the Soviet troops in Austria will help him to re-build a democratic Austria.
>
> 3. It should be made clear to Renner that the Soviet troops did not enter Austria to annex it but to get rid of Fascism.

There is little doubt that Renner was the man of the moment and carved for himself a unique place in European history. He set Austria on the road to freedom and his careful and well judged appeal to the Allies in 1919 at St Germain saved the Province of Carinthia. Like all Austrians he deplored the cession of South Tirol to Italy and after the Second World War, using his great experience and diplomacy, he set about trying to win back that Province. He alone among Austrian politicians knew how to play East against West. He knew too of the Carinthian problem and in 1945 while other politicians were finding it difficult to resolve the Yugoslav claims, Renner boasted that he had a letter in his pocket from Marshal Stalin which ensured that "Austria would never lose Carinthia".

By October Renner was completely disillusioned with the Russians and realised his provisional Government was nearing a crisis. He therefore decided to write a rather despairing letter to Foreign Minister Ernest Bevin:

> —— *I suppose that in no part of Europe such a mass of troops is concentrated as in the country which requires no military powers whether for its own protection or for the safety of the Allies. The saying has arisen here that an attempt is being made "to load four elephants in a rowing boat." The people of Austria cannot carry this fourfold burden for long without succumbing.*
>
> *Esteemed and honoured comrade! I beg your pardon for having had the audacity to bother you, who are entrusted with an abundance of tasks concerning all zones of the globe, with our small country and its four occupied zones. The fear of a catastrophe of my country prompts me to undertake this step and the fact that I am bound to you by the great idea of international collaboration of the labouring classes gives me the courage to appeal to you.*
>
> *Help our country, I beg of you, before it is too late.*

Bevin was sympathetic but waited until after the Austrian General Election on 25th November before responding on 30th November:

Dear Dr Renner,

1. I was very glad to receive your letter of the 16th October and would like to thank you for it and for the kind sentiments it contained.

2. You may be sure that I have read your letter with great sympathy. It is my sincere wish to do all I can to see that Austria is helped to regain true independence and prosperity.

Renner was only known to have lost his cool on one occasion when on 1st December, he had an outburst with the Chancellor of the Duchy of Lancaster in Vienna when he made an impassioned plea about his dependence on the Allies. When he wanted a litre of petrol he had to ask the Russians, bully beef he had to ask the United States etc. It was most unusual for him to speak so strongly on such matters. The reason for his conduct was apparently his recent "arrest" by the U.S. Military Police for speeding! Renner lived in Wahringerstrasse in the U.S. zone and the US had imposed a 25 mph speed limit because of safety aspects in this sector. Signs and warnings were displayed along the Wahringerstrasse but apparently Renner's driver completely ignored them. The car was stopped by the U.S. Military Police and Renner followed his driver into custody. The old man was furious and protested vigorously that he was the "first man in Austria". The plea went unheeded and it was two and a half hours before he was released.

The elections on 25th November held throughout Austria were the first free elections since 1930. A representative Government was formed under Chancellor Leopold Figl, who had spent five and a half years in Nazi concentration camps. Karl Renner was appointed President of Austria for a second time in his lifetime. Sadly Renner did not live to see the end of the occupation of his beloved Country for he died in office on the last day of 1950.

3

CONFLICT IN KLAGENFURT

After the Yugoslav invasion of 8th May, Marshal Tito's troops were soon spreading over Southern Carinthia and he decided to issue a proclamation through his Commander of the "Carinthian Military Zone":

> *The Yugoslav Army has arrived in Klagenfurt in order to liberate Carinthia from Nazi tyranny and to cleanse it from the Nazi tyrants. The whole area of liberated Carinthia is now under the military power of the Yugoslavian Army. Death to Fascism; Freedom to the people.*
>
> *Celovec, 12th May 1945*

Yugoslavia had made two armed incursions into Carinthia before, both after the First World War. While the Peace Conference was in session in Paris and in order to create a *fait accompli*, Yugoslavia invaded Carinthia on 29th April 1919. This was repelled by Austrian and Slovene Carinthian volunteers, but three weeks later the invasion was repeated and supported by a division of the regular Serbian army. Fighting took place all along a front from the valley of the Lavan to the valley of the Gail, and Klagenfurt was occupied by Yugoslav troops until July. At the same time Italian troops occupied the Villach – St Veit railway line in order to defend the Val Canale communication link.

The Province of Carinthia is surrounded by magnificent mountains rising in the North West to nearly 13,000 feet. These mountains, with their great jagged peaks and wooded foothills surround a beautiful Alpine valley dotted with lakes of which the Wörthersee, one of Austria's 800 lakes, is among the warmest in Europe. Practically the whole area of Carinthia is drained by the River Drau, or Drava, a large Alpine tributary of the Danube having a catchment area of some 16,000 square miles and an average flow of 11,000 million gallons per day (nearly nine times the flow of the Thames). In the south, the border with Yugoslavia is marked by the Karawanken range and with Italy by the Carnian and Julian Alps. Access over the Karawanken is by the Wurzen and Loibl passes and by rail through the Rosenbach tunnel. The mountains of Carinthia formed the Southern perimeter of Hitler's Alpine Redoubt ("Alpenfestung") where the Nazis planned to make their final stand. The Redoubt extended across the Alps from Salzburg in the north to Villach in the south and both towns were placed under the category of "Festungstädte" (fortified towns). About 80 per cent of the population of Carinthia is concentrated in the Drau Valley, in the towns of Klagenfurt, Villach and Lienz. The Province forms an ethnic transitional region between the Germanic north and Slav south. Slovenes had inhabited settlements in the area for centuries and it was these areas which were under dispute and which Yugoslavia referred to as "Slovene Carinthia".

Carinthia, even in 1945, had excellent lines of communications with both Italy and Yugoslavia in the south and Germany in the north. The road from Italy and the Adriatic to northeast Austria enters Carinthia from the Italian Val Canale centred on Tarvisio. This route has been, since ancient times, the main thoroughfare between Italy and Central and Eastern Europe crossing the great West-East European transversal line of the Danube Valley near Vienna. It is the route by which the main body of the Eighth Army entered Carinthia.

Marshal Tito was quick to announce his territorial claims:

1. The cession of the southern part of the Austrian Province Carinthia ["Slovene Carinthia"] amounting to an area of about "1,000 square miles and a population of some 180,000 people" [one fifth of the area of Carinthia and one half of the population].

2. A number of minor border rectifications in favour of Yugoslavia along the Austro-Yugoslav frontier area in the Austrian Province of Styria involving about "50 square miles of territory and about 10,000 people".

Today, the beautiful Drau Valley is one of Europe's tourist resorts. In the Spring of 1945 it was on the verge of becoming a battlefield. Tito had available to him six armies fully equipped with a strength of 50 divisions totalling half a million men. Of these, the Third Army was in Northern Slovenia and the Fourth Army in Venezia Giulia. Faced with the Russians in the east and Yugoslavs in the south, the British showed great restraint in a potentially explosive situation. It became clear that her policy would be shaped to maintain the peace, albeit a shaky one, and retain Carinthia's southern frontier pending a political settlement. British policy since the early days of the war had been to liberate Austria and maintain her 1937 frontier.

British troops of the 58 Regt. RA 6 British Armoured Division check their 4.5 inch guns in the main square (Neuer Platz) in Klagenfurt in preparation for possible engagement against Yugoslavia, 17th May 1945.

To the British public the war in Europe was over. Austria was a matter for the politicians but would British troops be willing to take up arms against their Yugoslav ally? There is no record of the British having considered appeasement in Carinthia, but to believe that Tito was bluffing was a risky option. Field Marshal Alexander considered the situation so dangerous that he instructed the planners to give him a full military appreciation, including the forces required to throw out the Yugoslavs. In a telegram to the Chief of Staff in London he asked:

> *In the event of hostilities against Yugoslavia, I must know on what divisions I can rely . . .*

But at the same time he was worried about the morale of his troops.

> *Before we are committed I think it as well to consider the feelings of our troops in this matter. They have a profound admiration for Tito's Partisan Army and a great sympathy for them in their struggle for freedom. We must be very careful therefore before we ask them to turn away from the common enemy to fight an ally.*

A British appreciation of the Yugoslav army strength showed that the Yugoslav resistance forces dated from autumn 1942 when a centralised command was instituted. Numbers under arms grew from 20,000 at the beginning of 1943 to 100,000 in August 1943 and 200,000 by the end of that year. Thirteen divisions and an armoured brigade were concentrated in the Fiume area in Istria and central Slovenia; five to seven divisions occupied north-west Slovenia and the Austrian frontier area and the remainder were distributed throughout other areas of Yugoslavia.

During their short occupation of Carinthia the Yugoslav Partisan Army created a situation for which the Eighth Army had not been prepared. Faced with their many other problems: food scarcity, prisoners of war, displaced persons, Cossacks and de-nazification, they carried a heavy responsibility. They were shaping history and would be so judged.

On arrival in Klagenfurt on the morning of 8th May, British troops lost no time in occupying most of the main public buildings. Yugoslav leaflets in both German and Slovene were printed in the offices of Klagenfurt's only newspaper, the Partisan's having requisitioned the building before the British could reach it. The British had to make do with a portable printing press on which they not only printed posters and leaflets but also the first free newspaper in Carinthia since the Anschluss. Most of the Yugoslav leaflets and posters ended with a proclamation signed by the "Commander of the Carinthian Military Zone":

> *The Yugoslav Army has established military power in free Carinthia.*

They were forced to rely on supplies solely through confiscation or force. In the village of Maria Saal, for example, they demanded a daily supply of 20 kilograms of meat and 40 kilograms of bread from the inhabitants and if their demands were not met they would simply rob the village.

They interned many helpless civilians on the pretext that they were Nazis and transported them to Yugoslavia. In the two weeks of their occupation it is known that some 90 people so arrested never returned. Needless to say by this time the attitude of the British troops had hardened towards the Partisans, much to the relief of the civilian population. Most Carinthians were still worried that the British would, under the severest pressure, give way to the Partisan demands and conduct a policy of appeasement. However, the Yugoslav venture into Carinthia, if anything, damaged Tito's territorial claims. The violent methods employed by his troops and their general behaviour were obnoxious even to his Carinthian sympathisers. Diplomatic pressure by Churchill and Truman to resolve the situation at last bore fruit and Tito agreed that, having made his point, he would now bow to diplomatic persuasion and take his claims to the Peace Conference. He would therefore withdraw his troops from Carinthia on 21st May but it was understood by Britain, the United States and the Soviet Union that the agreement in no way prejudiced the ultimate disposition of the Yugoslav territorial claim.

A similar agreement was made in connection with Venezia Giulia which placed the region to the west of a so called "Morgan Line" (named after General Morgan, Chief of Staff to Alexander) and the port of Pola, or Pula, under the Supreme Allied Commander. Yugoslav forces to the west of this line would be withdrawn by 12th June except for a detachment which would come under Alexander's control. The final settlement on Venezia Giulia however was not resolved until 1954 after considerable negotiation and international friction. The zone east of the Morgan Line, as well as Pula, went to Yugoslavia and the City of Trieste to Italy.

In order to make sure that the Yugoslavs withdrew from Carinthia according to the agreement and by the deadline fixed, the British helped to expedite matters by supplying trucks to transport the Partisans over the frontier.

One company of Partisans however remained at Behenbach until the 6th September and at Rosenbach until the 14th September with the excuse of providing escort duties for Yugoslav displaced persons. By the end of September, however, the last Partisan on Austrian soil had officially left Carinthia.

Yugoslav forces marching through Klagenfurt on their way out after agreeing to evacuate Carinthia (21st May 1945).

As soon as they had agreed to withdraw their troops, however, a propaganda war was waged from Belgrade. It started on the 20th May with an announcement on Yugoslav radio.

> *The intention of the Government to avoid misunderstandings with the allies was best shown by the example of Carinthia. Our Government at the appropriate moment asked the allies that they should take the Yugoslav army into consideration when fixing zones of occupation in Austria, especially Carinthia where the Slovene population was a furnace of resistance with Germany itself. The Soviet Union approved this demand of our Government. Meanwhile the allied Powers occupied the greater part of Carinthia, and our army, while still engaged in fighting the enemy, had at the allied request to*

hand over the campaign to the allied forces. Our Government accepted this demand. Our troops retired from Carinthia just as there is no doubt that the presence of the Yugoslav army in Trieste and in Julinska Krajina (Venezia Giulia) in no way prejudices the decisions of the Peace Conference. We underline that the withdrawal of our troops from Carinthia does not mean that our peoples will renounce their justified demand that this region, where the majority of the population is Slovene, should be incorporated in Democratic Federative Yugoslavia.

Smuggling of propaganda material in and out of Austria either for subsequent distribution in Carinthia or for use in Yugoslav press and radio was also a matter which concerned the British Military Government. The smuggling involved the use of a well organised courier and post-box system. The favourite route was through the Rosenbach rail tunnel and couriers frequently carried rucksacks full of newspapers and pamphlets by this route for distribution in Villach and Klagenfurt.

In order to control the frontier, the British introduced a Prohibited Frontier Zone (PFZ) being an imaginary line extending from the Gail Valley in the west to the Koralpe in the east and passing through Maria Gail, the Drau and Lippitzbach. In effect this line, with sentry posts appropriately located, pushed the international frontier north by several miles and facilitated both military and civil control. Illegal frontier crossings had become a serious problem. In a two week period in August thirty unauthorised persons were discovered in the PFZ of whom twenty had crossed illegally but this represented only a fraction of all unauthorised crossings. A Joseph Flatnitzer for example was arrested on his return from the Slovene Youth Congress in Ljubljana in June and admitted that eighteen people from Carinthia had attended the Congress and had crossed the frontier illegally.

There were four types of illegal crossings known to the British.

> 1. Inhabitants of the frontier area who for years were used to making short journeys for private or business purposes and who completely ignored the ban;

2. political couriers and agents of Yugoslav intelligence;

3. displaced persons from Yugoslavia;

4. people invited by Yugoslavia to attend political meetings.

To add to the problem, some 400 Austrian farmers, mainly in Styria, farmed land on both sides of the frontier amounting to about 7,500 acres ("Doppelbesitz").

Border crossings were, in general, being made for political agitation, propaganda, espionage and, in some cases, acts of violence. One such case concerned a Croat, who was working on a farm near Volkermarkt. Two armed Yugoslavs arrived at the farm on 30th June about 3 pm and asked the farmer's daughter the whereabouts of the Croat. She directed them to a field in which he was working where the Yugoslavs promptly shot him dead. They left as nonchalantly as they had come.

On another occasion, on 22nd July at 6 am, six young Austrians from Ferlach set out to climb the Kosutnikturm. They were seen on the summit at 9 am but shortly afterwards disappeared and were not seen again until 26th July. They had been arrested by a Yugoslav sentry and taken to Seeland (Yzerko) and thence to Neumarkt (Trzic). There they were interrogated as to the reasons for their presence on the frontier and questioned on conditions in Carinthia and relations between British troops and civilians. On the 24th July they were sent to Rodmansdorf and tried by a Yugoslav Military Court and accused of belonging to a secret Fascist organisation. The three girls were treated well but the boys were handled roughly and had their hands tied and were threatened. The six were acquitted and sent back to Austria via Stanna Krainburg (Kranj) and across the frontier at Hainsattel.

Frontier arrest by Yugoslav troops was not restricted to civilians, however, for in August and September 1946 four British soldiers disappeared at various times. Later it was learned that they had wandered over the frontier and were arrested. The frontier in places was difficult to define and the soldiers were not aware of its precise location. One of them had only strayed 100 yards inside Yugoslavia to buy wine. Despite overtures from the British Embassy in Belgrade, the British Authorities were refused visits to the soldiers and it was many months before they were released.

The plight of at least 40,000 Cossacks and 30,000 or so anti-Tito Yugoslavs captured by the British in Carinthia deserves special mention. After forty years of virtual silence this matter suddenly became a political issue in 1986 when Tolstoy published his book "The Minister and the Massacres". The Minister was Harold Macmillan, Lord Stockton, and the massacres were carried out by Stalin's Russia and Tito's Yugoslavia. In the book, Tolstoy claims that there is "no element of doubt" that Harold Macmillan was responsible for returning the Cossacks to Russia and the anti-Tito Yugoslavs (Croats, Ustasi, Chetniks and Slovenes) to Yugoslavia. Although pledges were given to Stalin at the Yalta Conference of the Big Three that the Cossacks would be repatriated, Tolstoy argues that this agreement did not include non-Soviet citizens or emigrés nor the Yugoslavs. Emigrés were those Russians who had been living abroad since the Russian Revolution and had acquired foreign nationality. The Soviet Commander in Styria, Marshal Tolbukhin, had explicitly reminded General Keightley, 5 Corps Commander, on 10th May at their meeting in Voitsberg, of the Yalta agreement and demanded the repatriation of the Cossacks.

In his diary for 13th May Macmillan wrote:

> . . . *with the Russians are considerable Bulgar forces. Moreover, among the surrendered Germans are about 40,000 Cossacks and "White" Russians, with their wives and children. To hand them over to the Russians is condemning them to slavery, torture and probably death. To refuse, is deeply to offend the Russians, and incidentally break the Yalta agreement. We have decided to hand them over (General Keightley is in touch and on good terms with the Russian general on his right), but I suggest that the Russians should at the same time give us any British prisoners or wounded who may be in his area.*

The history of the Cossacks covers a period of some 500 years involving communities scattered over 5,000 miles of Russia. They formed a distinctive ethnic group and came from the valleys of the Don (Don Cossacks), the Ural (Ural Cossacks), the Terek (Terek Cossacks) the Kuban (Kuban Cossacks) and other areas of the Soviet Union. They were hated by many Bolsheviks for their pro-Tsarist role and Stalin purged them incessantly. However when the Germans invaded Russia in 1941 most Cossacks in Russia rallied to the Soviet side. They may not have agreed with Stalin's Communism but they were patriots and loathed the Germans and some 100,000 Cossacks were in the Red Army at the outbreak of the war. Their gallantry at the gates of Moscow and Leningrad became a symbol of resistance and raised the morale of the army. Their heroism has passed into Russian history and although they suffered shocking losses, the Kuban Guards Cavalry Corps picked up the highest Soviet awards for gallantry in the war.

When the Germans occupied the area of the Don and Kuban rivers, a number of cossacks in these areas went over to the Germans and greeted the invaders with open arms, although the Germans turned down their first requests to form a Cossack Unit to help the Germans fight the Bolsheviks. However a Cossack Major, Kononov (later Colonel), deserted with his regiment and was pemitted by the Germans to form a squadron of Cossack deserters and prisoners of war. Kononov proceeded to feed propaganda into Russia in order to lure deserters over to the Germans and vowed to clear the Communist enemy off Russian soil.

In 1942 Hitler personally sanctioned the formation of volunteer Cossack units and in the Autumn of that year General Wagner approved the establishment of a self governing Cossack district in the Kuban region.

General Krasnov, former "Ataman" of the Don Cossacks, became an adviser of Cossack affairs and his views were compatible with Hitler's with respect to Bolshevism. His long association with Hitler and the Nazi cause enabled the Cossacks to establish a Nationalist Party in Prague whose members recognised the Führer as supreme dictator of the Cossack Nation. A central Cossack office was established in Berlin and prominent Cossack leaders such as Generals Shkuro, Naumenko and Domanov massed under the Nazi banner. They planned to extend the independent area in the Kuban and create a puppet state from the Ukraine to the Samara. They were taking a gamble and risking the wrath of Stalin and they knew it. But before these ambitious plans could be carried out the Germans were in retreat and the Cossacks with them. There was now no way out and they paid their last farewell to Russian soil with a trail of rape, looting and murder.

Meanwhile another Cossack division was formed under Colonel Pannwitz. It consisted of seven regiments, two each of the Don and

Kuban Cossacks and one each of the Terek and Siberian Cossacks and one mixed. The uniforms were German and only a badge distinguished them from the Wehrmacht soldier. They were sent to Yugoslavia to fight Tito's partisans. In order to raise morale they were fitted out with the Cossack fur caps and the traditional scarlet-striped trousers. Some of the younger Cossacks were even sent to Cavalry school in Germany. Domanov's Don Cossacks were moved to the foothills of the Italian Alps and early in 1945 some 10,000 Cossacks from the Don, Kuban and Terek arrived with their families in Tolmezzo with General Krasnov to set up a new Cossack State. They were not welcome by the local people and were accused of stealing food and property and shooting suspects in reprisals for partisan activity. They used what grazing there was for their horses and camels and were generally disliked. Faced with the Russians, the British and Tito's Yugoslavs all closing in on Austria, the Cossacks were cornered.

The Tolmezzo Cossacks were forced to move into Austria as the Eighth Army raced north and they entered Lienz on 4th May. It was the stragglers bringing up the rear of this Cossack retreat that the British met on the Plöcken Pass on 7th May.

The Cossacks now in retreat from the Russian and Yugoslav fronts moved up the Drau Valley and they too arrived in Lienz. The 30,000 Yugoslavs fleeing from Tito (as described by Tolstoy), moved across the frontier into Carinthia and surrendered to 5 Corps and were held in a huge camp at Viktring outside Klagenfurt. This number, however, did not include the quarter of a million Croat troops, half a million civilians and three hundred thousand German troops all of whom crossed into Carinthia to surrender or to seek protection from the British. It does, however, include the thousands massacred by Tito's partisans at Bleiburg on 15th May, a day that almost ended the independent State of Croatia.

> *I was living near Velden in "Slovene Carinthia" when the British troops entered Austria. Tito's partisans were already in the village when the Welsh Guards arrived and set up camp alongside the partisans to keep an eye on them. There was no trouble however and the detachment of partisans left when the main partisan forces retreated back into Yugoslavia on 21st May. During this period the Welsh Guards were also engaged in sending groups of*

> *Croats back to Yugoslavia. These Croats had fought against Tito during the war and had caused great stress to the partisans. Tito demanded their return and they knew that his revenge would be severe. The job for the British was a nasty one and I still remember a Welsh Guard's sergeant who was billeted with my parents sitting down to dinner one evening with tears running down his face. He had been involved in the day's forced transfer of Croats who had pleaded to remain in British captivity rather than face the wrath of Tito.*

Lienz had become the last rallying point for the Cossacks and it was there in May that they surrendered to the 2nd British Armoured Division.

Tolstoy maintains that Macmillan alone made the decision to repatriate the Cossacks and Yugoslavs but it is almost certain that both Alexander and Churchill knew of the "agreement" made in Klagenfurt. In fact Macmillan spent a long weekend at Chequers with Churchill the week after he had been to Klagenfurt but before leaving for England had "an hour's talk with Alex [Field Marshal Alexander C in C Mediterranean] on various last points."

On arrival at Northolt he drove direct to Chequers:

> *After dinner a short film, and then a lot of talk (till about 2 am) about Tito. I did my best to explain to PM the whole position as we saw it at AFHQ [Allied Forces Headquarters, Caserta, Italy] and all the various problems which we had to face locally.*

Macmillan remained at Chequers until the 22nd when he flew back to Caserta and spent the evening with Alexander. It would seem almost unbelievable that his visit to Klagenfurt was not discussed in detail at these meetings. Moreover Tolstoy's argument does not consider the mood and conditions of the period, nor the exigencies of war. British public opinion at the time was very pro-Russian and had little sympathy for those Cossacks who committed treason against their ally. With a powerful Russian army on the doorstep ready to support Tito's demands in Trieste and Carinthia, there existed a potentially explosive situation which could only be made worse by denying the Russians the return of the Cossacks and Tito the return of his enemies.

Many Cossacks, however, escaped from the Drau Valley when British troops may have turned a "blind eye". Most of them hid in the mountains and carried on a nomadic existence for many years until it was safe to settle down and start a new life again. One such Cossack who experienced these hardships and settled down in Carinthia, now runs a small business, but refused to discuss his experiences with the author nor allow his name to be used. He preferred to forget.

During the summer of 1945 General Keightley decided that some 8,000 Cossacks of the Drau Valley were neither Soviet citizens nor war criminals and ordered that they be sent across the frontier to a camp in Rimini in Italy. The Cossacks remained there unguarded with some 20,000 Ustasi and Chetniks until 1947 when, in accordance with the Italian Peace Treaty, British troops had to be withdrawn and foreign nationals suspected of having been war criminals transferred on demand for trial. In spite of demands from the Soviet Union for the return of these Cossacks, all 8,000 of them were "screened" and transported to Britain to a Scottish POW camp and later released. There the matter rested for nearly 40 years. In 1986, the Simon Wiesenthal Center in Los Angeles informed the British Government that it was probable that many of those entering the United Kingdom in 1947 may have been war criminals and certainly had been members of the SS police units.

Others, however, did not have the same luck. Karasov and his colleagues were found guilty of armed struggle, espionage and terrorist activities against the Soviet Union by a Soviet Military Court and hanged in 1947. With them went Shkuro, Domanov and Von Pannwitz. Thousands spent the rest of their lives in Gulags throughout the Soviet Union and a few of those who were set free under Krushchev's Amnesty Decree of 1955 returned to Carinthia to live out the rest of their lives.

An independent committee of inquiry was set up to investigate Tolstoy's charges. This committee under the chairmanship of Brigadier Anthony Cowgill spent two years considering Tolstoy's allegations and in doing so traced the documents that Tolstoy maintained were either lost or had been removed. The committee reported in September 1988 and completely exonerated Macmillan.

Macmillan left Italy for good four days later to become Secretary of State for War. On 13th May 1955, exactly ten years to the day after his Klagenfurt meeting he arrived in Vienna as British Foreign Minister to sign the Austrian State Treaty. Two years later he became Prime

Minister. In 1980 he was invited back to Austria for the twenty-fifth anniversary of the signing of the Treaty. Macmillan was an immensely compassionate man and the allegations about his role in the repatriation of the Cossacks and Yugoslavs hurt him deeply. He was certain, however, that in time he would be vindicated. Unfortunately he did not live to hear the verdict which cleared him of all Tolstoy's allegations.

The final guilt for this blood-stained episode in our history must rest with Marshal Joseph Vissarionovich Stalin and Marshal Josip Broz Tito.

Meanwhile Tito's propaganda war continued, and on 20th July fifty copies of *Ljudska Pravica* marked *"Celovec"* (Klagenfurt) were found by British Field Security personnel. A rubber dinghy was found for transporting the papers across the Drau, and in a house near Rosenbach an account was found for 12,500 newspapers from Ljubljana.

Whilst the PFZ never completely stopped illegal frontier crossings, it served its purpose as a deterrent and continued to be effective until it was lifted in 1949.

Yugoslav radio and newspapers, however, continued to pour out propaganda almost daily during the following months. On 25th May *Tanjug* "reported":

> *After the liberation of all Carinthia numerous meetings and reunions were held at which the Slovenians and Austrians from Carinthia manifested their attachment to Tito's Yugoslavia. Everywhere the Carinthians demanded to be returned to Yugoslavia.*

And on 26th May the same newspaper reported that units of the Allied police and those of the former "Carinthian Hitlerite Government" were carrying out arrests of the Slovene Partisans in Klagenfurt and that the people of Carinthia demanded their annexation to Tito's Yugoslavia. On the same day the paper reported that the Allied Military Police and other British troops surrounded a house in Klagenfurt on the 23rd of May in which was located the headquarters of the Slovene National Liberation Committee for Slovene Carinthia. The paper went on to claim that the police units searched the house in an "extraordinary and cruel manner" and all members of the Committee present were arrested. In continuing its propaganda attack the newspaper contended that the police also broke into a printing press in Klagenfurt where Slovene and anti-Fascist papers were printed and removed the people inside and sealed off the premises. The paper alleged that the local police involved were former Gestapo members.

On the 28th May, *Tanjug* reported Marshal Tito's speech in Ljubljana in which he said:

> *Only a few days have passed since our troops were obliged to leave Carinthia and already we hear the cries of our Carinthian brethren and their shouts for help.*

Barba on 29th May accused the British of closing their eyes while the Nazis persecuted the Yugoslav fighters for national liberty. The paper referred to the "Nazi Government at Klagenfurt" and the British support for it.

Tass reported that in Celovec and Beljak (Villach) and other towns, armed Medices, Ustashi and SS men who pinned the British military badge on their Gestapo uniforms freely walked the streets. The population is in "depressed spirits", the paper alleged, and the people ask "what will happen now? When will this terror end?"

The *Slovenski Procevalec* published on 1st June a declaration of the Vice President of the Slovene National Liberation Committee for Slovene Carinthia:

> *While the Yugoslav Army was leaving Carinthia, people wept in the streets and begged the soldiers to remain. The Provisional Regional Government in Klagenfurt is pro-Fascist and incapable of solving any problems whatsoever.*

Pravda published an article on or about 3rd June claiming that a *Tass* correspondent reported in a despatch that a delegation of the Slovene National Liberation Committee for Slovene Carinthia requested that the population of Carinthia be protected from violence and atrocities to which they were being subjected. They said that all sorts of Fascist scum, beginning with former SS men down to Quislings headed by the "executioner of the Slovenian people, Rupnik, Catholic Bishop of Rojman and others, found not only shelter but are also given the full freedom of action in Carinthia." "Many SS men, White Guards and Nedice gangsters", the correspondent claimed, "had been enlisted by the British Military Government into the police and gendarmery set up in Carinthia. Protected by the administration, they committed unheard of crimes against the newly-born democracy against Austrians and especially against the Slovenian population of Carinthia. This terror was especially intensified when, complying with the demands of the British, Yugoslav troops moved out of Carinthia which they had entered pursuing German troops routed by them in Yugoslavia."

In a speech on 4th June at Ledjce Marshal Tito declared:

Carinthia is ours . . . and we shall fight for her.

Also on 4th June *Tanjug* reported that Marshal Tito received a delegation of the people of Slovene Carinthia on 1st June who declared that after the departure of the Yugoslav Army, a reign of terror was carried out in Carinthia by former Fascist elements. On the same day *Barba* contained an article on "a review of the Fascist reign of terror that is now in full swing in Carinthia". In view of these and other reports and accusations appearing in the Yugoslav Press concerning the situation in Carinthia since the withdrawal of Yugoslav troops, the British Authorities felt called upon to respond and a Press Release on 21st June declared that:

Up to 7th June, 1945, 732 arrests were made in Carinthia on security grounds, of whom all but 36 were officials under the Nazi régime. The remaining 36 were all arrested on various grounds of security within the existing directives of the Allied Military authorities on the spot. Out of the total of 732, only 6 were Yugoslavs, all of whom had been employed by the Germans. A further 345 persons were arrested for civil offences against the Military Government, such as contravention of the curfew and movement regulations, and 134 were arrested for ordinary crimes, mostly theft.

The action taken against members of the Slovene National Liberation Committee was purely military, in accordance with operational orders regarding the withdrawal of Yugoslav troops from the area. It had no political significance whatsoever. The civilians concerned (who, it is alleged, were arrested) were in fact Yugoslavs who, after questioning by the Military security authorities, were escorted the same day to the Yugoslav frontier. The same is the case with the printing press which was closed down. It was closed when the Yugoslav troops were withdrawn, and the action had no political flavour.

When British troops entered Klagenfurt on 8th May, the Provincial Government which had been set up three days previously and taken over from Gauleiter Rainer who was forced to resign, offered its services to the Allied Military Government and, quite apart from the removal and replacement of Nazi officials, ceased to exercise any authority. On 28th May, the Allied Military Government formally announced that the Provincial Government was not recognised, and on 5th June the establishment of a consultative Committee was announced, which included well known anti-Nazis.

All members were first approved and vetted by Allied Military Government authorities, and a sharp watch kept for any persons who in the past had favoured a policy of pan-Germanism. One of the 12 members on this Committee represents the Slovene minority. Moreover Petek, the leader of the Slovene minority, was given a special pass to travel from his home to Klagenfurt at any time, and the Allied Military Government Officer in the area personally invited Petek to see him on Slovene minority matters whenever he wished, or alternatively to make any complaints he wished to the local Military Government Officer. No complaints were made.

A thorough de-Nazification of the local police was carried out. All special Nazi police formations were dissolved, and their personnel rounded up. All persons retained were carefully vetted, in consultation with experienced British police officers, and a strict check was maintained on them.

No local Slovenes were deported from Carinthia; the only cases of deportation were of Yugoslav Slovenes falsely claiming to be local. Widespread enquiries following upon the victimisation of the Slovene minority, and statements to this effect were without foundation, being based on false information. The Allied Military Government in Carinthia was as anxious as the Yugoslavs to wipe out Nazi influence there and to abolish the idea of pan-Germanism.

The Yugoslav propaganda campaign continued for the remainder of the year although its abrasiveness diminished slightly as the Yugoslav Government prepared its case for presentation to the Conference of Foreign Ministers.

4

THE DISPUTED FRONTIER

Yugoslavia had disputed the Slovene-Carinthia frontier ever since the new State of Yugoslavia emerged after the First World War. Large numbers of Slovene Carinthians lived in the border areas of Carinthia and Styria, particularly in the Drau Valley. Slovenes had settled there as early as the year 600 AD. They were of peasant stock drawn into a civilisation which had spread from the monastries and experienced the development of the feudal system, the rise of chivalry and the establishment of towns and market. Many settled in Klagenfurt and Villach and gradually took over the new institutions from the Germans and adopted German names for them. The two races blended well, and since German culture was wider it kept the upper hand.

A mixed language of German and Slovene, known as "Windisch", sprang up in this region and is still spoken today in Southern Carinthia. It is for this reason that in Austria the region gets the name the "mixed language area" in preference to "Slovene Carinthia" used by Yugoslavia. The people in the area prefer to use Windisch at home or in conversation with their neighbours and especially when referring to their animals, although there is a distinction here too because Windisch is used for names of cows or cats whereas German names are usually reserved for horses and dogs which they class as domestic animals because they appeared later. The Slovenes therefore, rightly or wrongly, considered Carinthia as the "cradle of their national culture".

> *Oh Slovenes where are your borders*
> *Oh Slovenes where is your blood*
> *There, at Gorica, there are our borders*
> *There, at Celovec, there is our blood.*

The original demand by Yugoslavia after the First World War extended to the whole of Carinthia to be included in the new State of Yugoslavia. Immediately after the Second World War, this claim was reduced to the one thousand square miles of Carinthian territory and fifty square miles of Styrian territory referred to in the previous chapter. However on 17th November the Yugoslav Ambassador to Britain met Mr Ernest Bevin in London and presented Yugoslavia's official claim – 350 square miles of Carinthian territory with the River Drau as the new frontier. This claim was accompanied by, what Yugoslavia considered, substantial reasons both historical and political which the British Government should accept as being fair and reasonable. Further, it was emphasised that Austrians were enthusiastic supporters of the Anschluss and fought for Hitler and that Nazism was still strong in Carinthia. It was contended also that the attempted Nazi revolution of 1934 had its centre in Carinthia and Styria.

The tablet on the Villach - Faak road marking both the territorial frontier of Autria - Yugoslavia claimed by Marshal Tito at the end of the Second World War and the 1920 Plebiscite Zone.

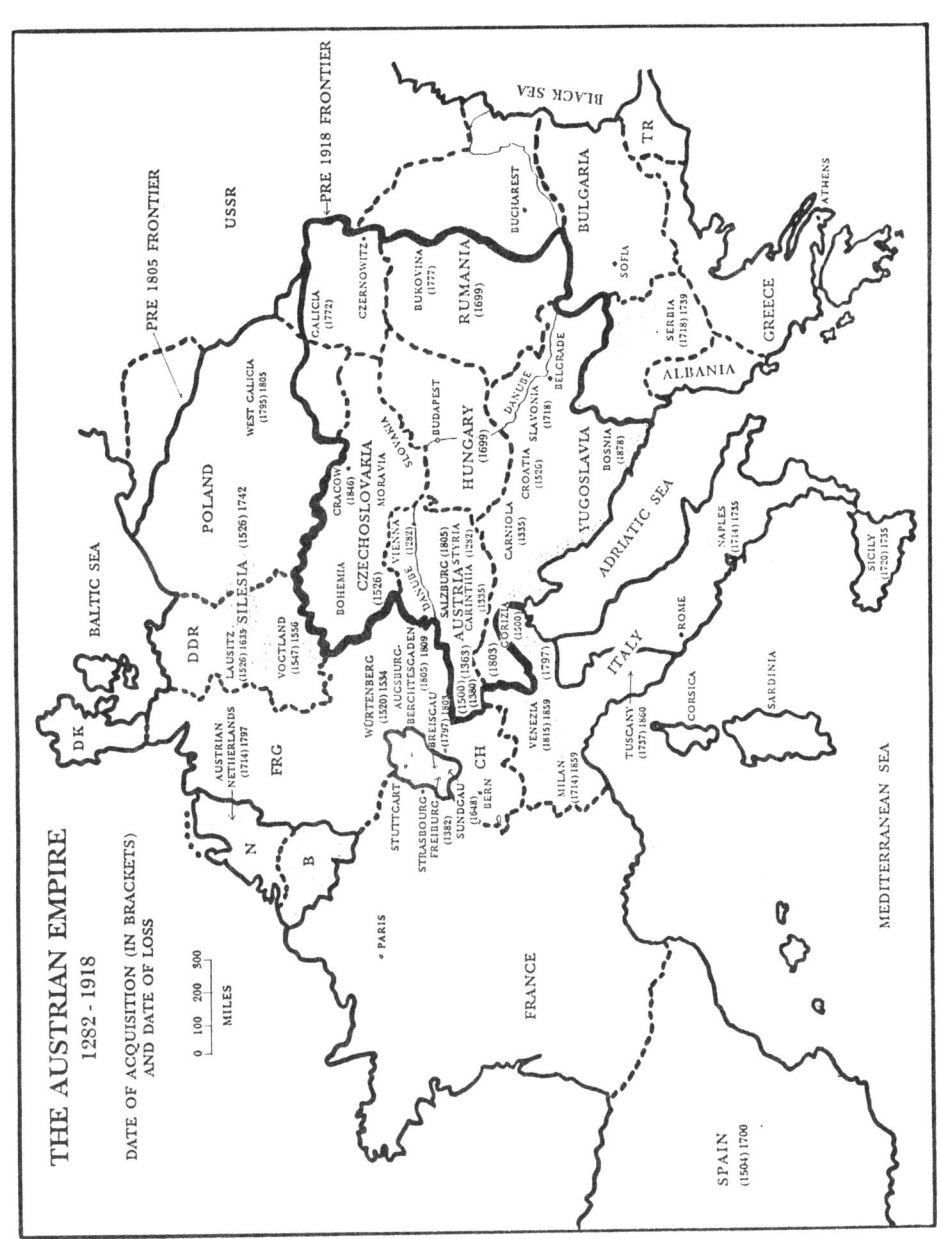

The situation, however, gave rise to rumour and conjecture in Carinthia especially in the areas likely to be affected. In Villach, on the Drau, which had always been a frontier town, the mood was such that people became almost resigned to a frontier change. Would the town be inside or outside Austria? Would it be divided? These were the questions they asked and it scared them:

> *I was born and brought up in Villach and during the winter of 1945/46 the radio and newspaper coverage of the Yugoslav claims were something I won't forget. We were relying on the British to resist the Yugoslavs but we couldn't be sure. The Yugoslav plan to divide the town so that east of the river would be Austria and west would be Yugoslavia created widespread fear. Today the very thought seems unreal but in the mood of the time it created great anxiety. Crossing the Drau bridge in town, as I often had occasion to do, I would stop and cast an eye towards the south to the Karawanken range and beyond and wonder when and where would it all end. What would happen to Villach, to Carinthia. The memory of those traumatic days has never left me.*

Historically the Yugoslav claim to Austrian territory originated after the First World War. At St Germain-en-Laye, near Paris, where the Peace Conference was held, the Austro-Hungarian Empire was broken up and the new States of Czechoslovakia, Hungary and Yugoslavia emerged. The former regions of Bohemia Moravia, Austrian Silesia, South Tirol, Val Canale, Carniola (Krain), Mies Valley, Seeland, Unterdrauburg (Dravograd) and Southern Carinthia (excluding Villach) were ceded outright by Austria to the Allies for their subsequent disposal. Weissenfels, which originally belonged to the Province of Carniola was claimed by Austria since it was populated by an overwhelming German speaking population and was economically dependent on Carinthia. But it was ceded to Italy by the Treaty of Rapallo after having been occupied by Yugoslav troops until 1920.

In the draft treaty handed to the Austrian delegation on 2nd June 1919, no plebiscites were included and Southern Carinthia was ceded to Yugoslavia. It was Dr Karl Renner who protested against these decisions:

putting millions of German-Austrians under a foreign domination against their will
and cited the Wilson principles.

Renner asked for plebiscites for Bohemia, Moravia, Austrian Silesia, South Tirol, Styria, Carniola and Carinthia. The Allies turned him down except in the case of Carinthia and Articles 49 and 50 were accordingly added to the Treaty of St Germain for a plebiscite to be held.

For the purpose of the plebiscite, the disputed area was divided into two zones: Zone 1, the Southern and larger zone followed a line south of Villach, and Velden, along the centre of the Wörthersee and south of Klagenfurt. This zone covered an area of 622 square miles with a population of some 73,000 who were apparently predominantly Slovene speakers. It was occupied by Yugoslav troops in the run up to the plebiscite. Zone 2 had an area of 133 square miles with a population of 54,000 and included the town of Klagenfurt. It was occupied by Austrian troops. The split of Slovene to German-speaking inhabitants in the two zones gave a clear advantage in Zone 1 to Yugoslavia:

	Zone 1	Zone 2
German	23,000	49,000
Slovene	50,000	4,500

The plebiscite in Zone 1 was held on 10th October 1920 under the control of the Interallied Plebiscite Commission whose President was the British Officer Lieutenant Colonel Peck. It resulted in a win for Austria, by 22,025 votes to 15,278 to the bitter surprise and disappointment of Yugoslavia. Austria therefore won 59 per cent of the votes against Yugoslavia's 41 per cent and since Austria won an overall majority the vote in the second zone was abandoned, as the treaty had provided, and minority clauses were added to the treaty. The plebiscite was a severe blow to Yugoslavia especially since the result in the districts south of the Drau gave her a 51 per cent majority – and Austria had argued unsuccessfully at the Peace Conference for the Drau to be taken as the line between the zones.

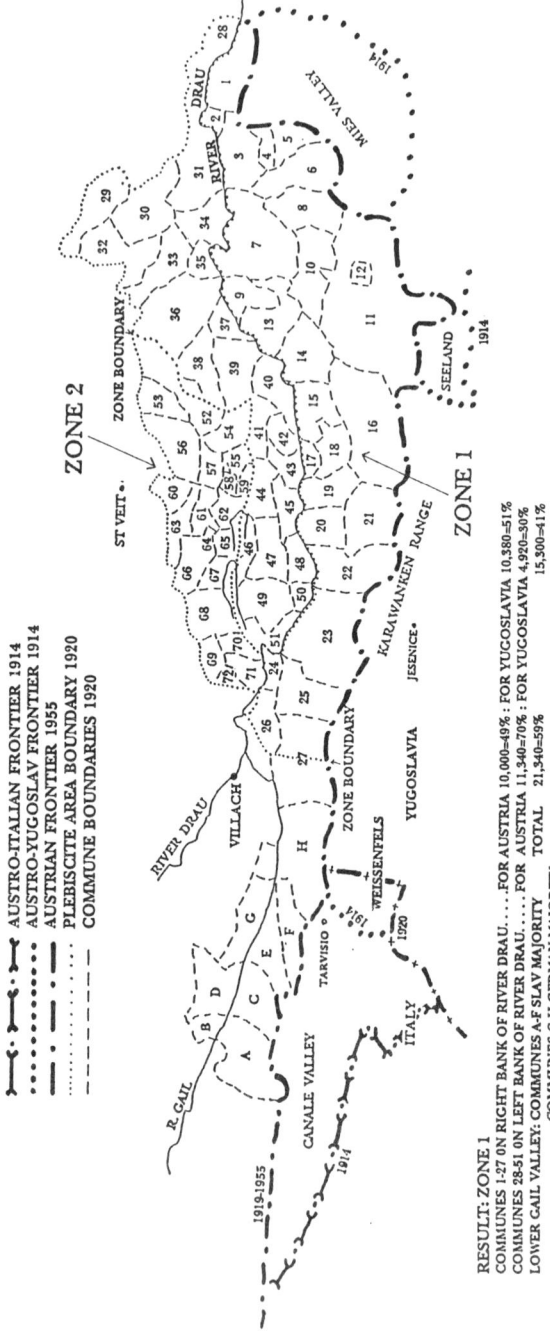

The Allied Supreme Council made one final concession to Austria when they ceded to her Western Hungary, now Burgenland. Sopron remained in Hungary, however, as a result of a disputed plebiscite in 1921. Further plebiscites (though unofficial) were held in Vorarlberg in 1919 and in Tirol and Salzburg in 1921. Vorarlberg voted by 47,208 votes to 11,248 for union with Switzerland and Tirol voted by 145,302 votes to only 1,805 against, for union with Bavaria. Salzburg followed with 103,000 votes for union with Bavaria and only 800 against.

The Allied Powers refused to accept all three results. Union with Germany was forbidden under the Treaties of Versailles and St Germain and the French did not wish a union of Vorarlberg with Switzerland lest it should interrupt the French-German balance there. Moreover the Allies considered that Austria had ceded enough territory from an empire of 60 million people which before 1914 had extended across central Europe from Lake Garda, now in Italy, to Czernowitz (Cernovcy) now in the Soviet Union. Nevertheless Austrian politicians, including Renner, did not consider that what was left after dismemberment was a viable economic State and the seeds of the Anschluss were sown. Yugoslavia warned, however, that the result of the 1920 plebiscite would be declared null and void should Austria ever enter into a union with Germany. Under such circumstances, Yugoslavia would renew her demand for the whole territory of Slovene Carinthia originally claimed at the Paris Peace conference.

Since Britain was directly responsible to the Allies for considering these claims, the Provincial Government of Carinthia submitted two Memorandums of appeal to the British Military Government in Klagenfurt.

> *The advance of the Tito troops in the first days of May, their attitude towards the population, the express statements made by them when they retired from Kärnten (Carinthia) and, most of all, the underground propaganda maintained by agents of Yugoslav nationality in the aforementioned parts of the country prove that the Yugoslav aspirations are to be taken very seriously.*

> *Although the Government of Kärnten has the fullest faith in the repeated declarations of the Allied Governments to the effect that Austria should be restored as a free and independent State within her frontiers of 1938, the*

Government feels it incumbent on them to call the special attention of the British Military Government for Austria to the fact that any modification of the Austrian Southern frontier of 1938 which might curtail her territory in favour of Yugoslavia, would gravely affect the economic and political vitality not only of Kärnten but of the entire Federation. Even a prolonged state of uncertainty as to the future frontiers of Austria would greatly hamper the return to normal conditions of life.

Therefore they urgently request the British Military Government of Austria to bring the considerations laid down in the present memorandum to the knowledge of His Britannic Majesty's Government and their Allies in order to use them as a basis for peace negotiations.

The Austrian contention was that the frontier having been established in 1920, relations between the two countries became normal and friendly. The new frontier did not of course correspond to the hopes and wishes of either side. Yugoslavia had to renounce the incorporation of the Slovenes of Carinthia while Austria, apart from the loss of the Mies District, had given up a far greater number of German-speaking Styrians, who formed the majority in the towns and boroughs of Southern Styria which had been handed over without plebiscite to Yugoslavia (mainly the Marburg area).

Austria maintained, however, that the new frontier was in the ensuing two decades one of the quietest in Europe. There was only one inconvenience of the frontier which was keenly felt in Austria, namely the interruption of the two lines of railway communication between Carinthia and Styria: the line Bleiburg-Maribor(Marburg)-Graz, which ran from Prävali to Spielfeld on Yugoslav territory and between Klagenfurt and Lavamünd, which crossed Yugoslav territory on the section Prävali-Unterdrauburg(Dravograd)-Lavamünd. The difficulties were only part removed by the agreement of both parties. Austria asserted that not until the Nazi propaganda began to spread on both sides of the frontier had the Yugoslav Government reason to be alarmed. But when Austria succumbed as the first victim of the Third Reich, the situation changed completely.

When war broke out between the Reich and Yugoslavia in April 1941, Austria had already ceased to be master of its own destiny. After the collapse of the Nazi régime in Austria in May 1945 the Provisional Government contended that it did its best to make reparations for the injuries that the régime had inflicted on the population of Slovenia and on the Slovenes of Carinthia.

Yugoslavia used every political trick available to prepare a case for the London Conference in January 1947 when the Carinthian question was on the Agenda of the Deputy Foreign Ministers' meeting in Lancaster House. Just before the conference opened it was announced that General Löhr had been tried by Tito for war crimes committed in Yugoslavia, found guilty and executed. During the conference they blatantly accused one of the Austrian delegates of having collaborated with the Nazis and demanded his expulsion from the meeting. He was Hans Piesch, Landeshauptmann of Carinthia. Britain and America, although certain that Piesch was innocent, were forced to agree with the demand and Piesch had to retire from the Austrian delegation and later resign his position as Landeshauptmann.

At the next London meeting of the Deputies in 1948, it is believed that the Yugoslavs had prepared yet another war crimes file accusing a member of the Austrian delegation. The member had been an aide to the Austrian Foreign Minister Karl Gruber at the 1947 meeting and had been expected to attend the 1948 meeting in the same capacity. However some four weeks before the meeting was due to start the aide had been moved to the Austrian Legation in Paris and was not present in London. His name was Kurt Waldheim.

The claims and counter claims of the frontier under dispute continued without being resolved. However in a last effort to seek a solution, Yugoslavia presented a final modified demand to a session of the London Treaty Conference in February 1949.

1. Rectification of the Austro-Yugoslav border in favour of Yugoslavia to a degree to be determined later on the basis of a compromise proposal.

2. Political, cultural and economic autonomy for that part of Slovene Carinthia that would continue to form a part of the Austrian Republic; the autonomy statute to be guaranteed by the Security Council of the United Nations.

3. Substantial reparations to be paid by Austria to Yugoslavia.

4. A guarantee of minority rights for those Croats and Slovenes who would remain ouside the autonomous area.

The areas whose cession by Austria were still sought were not specified in this, the last, Yugoslav claim. Moreover the areas which were to be included in the autonomous districts were unspecified but Yugoslavia declared that the autonomy should extend to the legislative, administrative and judiciary power and include the security of Slovenes.

The basic question for a political settlement of the Slovene Carinthia problem concerned the real ethnic situation in the contested areas. This had three aspects: the total number of Slovenes in Carinthia, their geographical distribution among the districts and communes and their national feelings. All these aspects were controversial between the two parties. Austria denied the existence of any compact Slovene settlement in Carinthia and based their claim, in general, on the figures of the 1934 census. Yugoslavia claimed that whatever might have been the value of these figures, it was nullified by the result of the 1939 German census, reference to which Austria avoided in their statement to the London Treaty Conference. Moreover Yugoslavia claimed that even the German figures might not represent the true picture because every Slovene who registered as such during the German occupation did so in the face of the enemy.

Yugoslavia concluded that the actual number of Slovenes in Carinthia was unknown as was also their geographical distribution. Their national feelings were also unknown but Yugoslavia claimed that it would be understandable if the persecutions and atrocities suffered by them at the hands of the German occupation had resulted in a sharpening of their national consciousness. However, in order to answer the questions posed by the unusual ethnic situation, Yugoslavia was against a plebiscite. A plebiscite, it was contended, presupposed a certain knowledge of the ethnic data necessary to determine which areas should be included in it, and in what groupings. They suggested therefore a fact finding mission headed by experts who were thoroughly familiar with European conditions and who were neutrals.

The prestige of plebiscites had waned since the First World War and frequently the vote in a plebiscite was influenced by temporary conditions as was the vote in periodical elections. The difference was that, while in the latter, the vote could be reversed in a subsequent election, the result of a plebiscite was final and permanent. The fate of a disputed territory was therefore determined even though the conditions responsible for the vote might change.

The Yugoslavs pointed to territorial issues having been settled since the end of the Second World War without resorting to plebiscites, some of them even contrary to the results of the plebiscites carried out under the treaties concluded at the end of the First World War. Examples they quoted included decisions in regard to the Saar and the Prussian areas of Marienwerder and Allenstein.

Yugoslavia may have considered that had Austria gained South Tirol and also the Canal Valley (Val Canale) she might well have agreed to the cession of a group of say ten or twelve border communes in the south east corner of Carinthia where there was a substantial majority for Yugoslavia in 1920. Austria, however, was sent away from the Italian Treaty Conference empty-handed. The French Foreign Minister moreover admitted that the failure of the Italian Treaty Conference to grant Austria any territorial relief at the expense of Italy made it humanly impossible for Austria to consider any similar concession in favour of Yugoslavia.

There now seemed little possibility that the Foreign Ministers would agree to even the modified Yugoslav demands. They agreed, however, to guarantee the rights of the Slovenes and Croat minorities in Carinthia, Burgenland and Styria and this would be written into the Austrian State Treaty.

There was still one frontier dispute to be considered by the Peace Conference, albeit a minor one. It concerned the Berchtesgaden area bordering Bavaria. Shortly after the war it was reported that the United States Government considered desirable the transfer of the Berchtesgaden region to Austria. This region forms a pocket wedged into the territory of the Salzburg Province with which it was closely connected until the Napoleonic era. Napoleon took the area from Austria and gave it to his ally, the King of Bavaria. After 1814 Austria was able to recover Salzburg, but not Berchtesgaden. In winter this area forms the only road link between east and west Austria since the other road connection is then impassable. The Berchtesgaden wedge also forces the railroad from Vienna via Salzburg-Tirol to Switzerland to a detour of about 100 miles. General Clark submitted a memorandum to the Austrian Treaty Conference regarding the imperative necessity to remedy the Berchtesgaden situation in favour of Austria. However, the Peace Conference decided that no action was necessary other than to permit transit facilities.

The political argument on Slovene Carinthia, however, would continue before the situation was finally resolved peacefully by the Austrian State Treaty as we shall see in Chapter 9.

British policy, however, supported the pre-Anschluss frontier and it gradually became clear that the only way Yugoslavia could gain Carinthian territory was by force. That had been tried and failed, due to British resistance.

Minority protection by Austria of the Slovene Carinthians however was declared by Dr Karl Renner in a speech he gave to a special session of the Diet of Carinthia held on 9th October 1950, just two months before he died, to commemorate the 30th anniversary of the plebiscite:

> *We want peace with our neighbour to the southeast. We do not want the general unrest in Europe and the world to produce disturbances at this, our border, again. It is with sincere sympathy that we are following Yugoslavia's struggle for existence, and we entertain but one wish; that the friendly relations, which were fortunately re-established after the final settlement of differences inherited from former days, may remain undisturbed by the troubles of our time and last for all time to come. May the finally secured border serve only to prevent any interference of one country in the internal affairs of the other, but not as a dividing wall; may it rather serve as a bridge for economic co-operation and cultural exchange. It is in this spirit and in no other that Austria and Carinthia are celebrating the anniversary of the plebiscite.*

Yugoslavia refused to acknowledge the anniversary celebrations and always contended that, in 1938, when Hitler invaded Austria and declared the Anschluss, the result of the 1920 plebiscite was null and void.

5

RESISTANCE

On 6th April 1941 Nazi Germany in alliance with Italy and Bulgaria attacked Yugoslavia and within a few weeks the country was overrun. Yugoslavia was then partitioned, the southern part of Slovenia including Ljubljana going to Italy while Germany augmented "Reichsgau" Carinthia with northern Carniola. Southern Styria was added to "Reichsgau" Styria.

Mass denationalisation, deportation and extermination were reported to have taken place. It is claimed that the Nazis deported as many as 2,000 Slovene patriots from Carinthia to Germany for slave labour and into concentration camps and a further 2,000 families deported to the interior of Germany. Before long, however, underground partisan resistance centres sprung up in several parts of Carinthia. The conditions for partisan activities were difficult because Carinthian Slovenes capable of carrying arms were mobilised in the German army and it was dangerous to desert and join the partisans because of the massive German garrisons in Carinthia. Moreover severe reprisals on the civilian population were carried out should they be caught taking part in resistance activities.

However in spite of the growing disillusion in Austria no significant purely Austrian resistance emerged on a wide scale. Gestapo control, popular reaction against Tito "bandits", the absence of the young and the failure of the inter-war Austrian Republic to produce a strong national consciousness, all combined to render abortive the numerous small attempts to organise anti-Nazi feeling into open resistance. Right up to the immediate pre-collapse period, the only known openly active anti-Nazi elements were the Slovene Carinthian partisans and a small group of Italian partisans in the Tarvisio area, just across the Austrian frontier.

There was an attempt by the British after the surrender of the German Africa Korps in 1943 to recruit some anti-Nazi Austrian agents to drop into Austria. Some thirty former Austrian prisoners of war volunteered for training with SOE in Southern Italy, and in February-March 1945 four blind drops were made into Austria. In the last 6 weeks of the war over 20 of these SOE agents were dropped, but they had little time to achieve results of importance.

There was, however, an interesting report of a social democrat with underground experience in Styria who was conscripted into the Wehrmacht in 1944 and decided to desert to the Maquis in France. He volunteered to return to Austria and he and his party organised an effective group based at Bad Aussee. When the United States army arrived he was able to hand over to them an already effective local administration. He also helped to arrest Kaltenbrunner and other top SD officers and to recover the Austrian Crown Jewels and other property of great value.

There were many cases of sabotage in Austria reported by the Gestapo as well as the use of the indirect weapons of "go slow", "work to rule" and absenteeism. Austria also played an important part in the 20th July (1944) plot to murder Hitler, and in Vienna at the given signal many leading Nazi Party and Gestapo officials were arrested and key buildings seized. The failure of the plot led to many Austrians being rounded up and either imprisoned or sentenced to death. Leopold Figl the future Chancellor was one who was involved and found himself in a concentration camp.

The Nazi Herrenvolk (superiors) in Carinthia were distrustful of the local people. After the July plot, all members of the Landtag of Carinthia were arrested and some sent to Dachau. Great numbers of German officials had already been imported to ensure that Nazi authority was firmly established.

In the Autumn of 1944 a resistance group known as "05" sprung up in Vienna. "05" represented the first two letters in "Oesterreich", the "5" being the fifth letter of the alphabet "e". Towards the end of the war most Austrians recognised "05" as the code sign for resistance and the sign could be found chalked up on buildings all over Austria. This group established contact with the Allies in Switzerland and performed some useful preparatory work for the liberation.

Although Austrian resistance was relatively minor compared with that in other occupied countries the difficulties were greater. Language was a problem too because Austrians spoke German and this made things easier for the Gestapo and the police. Informers with divided loyalties were numerous. In spite of these difficulties it is estimated that nearly 36,000 Austrian resistance fighters were either executed or died in Gestapo prisons.

We shall probably never know, therefore, the full story of Austrian resistance during the Nazi era but it is most likely that it has been underestimated and undervalued. However, we are aware of many exploits by resistance leaders and supporters which proved successful in spite of consistent penetration of cells due mainly to the burden of the common language. It was also unfortunate that the 70,000 victims rounded up throughout Austria immediately after the Anschluss included almost all the leaders of the nation. The Defence Minister was murdered with 20 generals and one third of the general staff dismissed.

Nevertheless, passive resistance actually started on the morning of Hitler's invasion. This took root when the first cell was formed by a group of NCOs in Vienna under the leadership of Sergeant Franz Studeny. By 1943 his network merged with another patriotic movement led by Major Szokoll. Their aim was to disrupt army plans, orders and postings but the group will be remembered most for its active participation in the July plot to murder Hitler. When the news was first telegraphed to Vienna, members of the group immediately arrested and disarmed the key Nazi commanders in the capital, but just as Szokoll was about to proclaim the liberation of Austria, the news of the failure of the plot was flashed to the city. In the next few hours hundreds were seized and imprisoned in Nazi gaols.

Of those executed was the chief of regional military intelligence, Colonel Court Marogna-Redivitz. Szokoll only just survived and by the beginning of 1945 he had organized patriotic field units around Vienna by falsifying army movements and returns. Commanders of these units included Colonel Franz Hofer, Major Schick and Major Biedermann. Probably one of the most active of all political resistance fighters was Dr Hans Becker. The objectives of cells under his control included normal sabotage but also cooperation with underground groups in neighbouring countries. By the end of the war membership of his organisation had reached nearly 15,000 and liaison was established with 05. One of the young Austrian leaders, Fritz Molden, played a significant role in this group and travelled widely recruiting members and opening up communication channels. Towards the end of the war Molden made contact with the Western Allies in Italy and had lengthy talks with Alexander's staff in his headquarters in Caserta. As a result of these talks, the Western Allies agreed to arms deliveries to partisans and to drops of US liaison officers in Tirol.

One of the most remarkable resistance cells was operated by Hubert Sauerwein, an engine driver from the Ötztal, an anti-Nazi Tirolian valley near Innsbruck. Sauerwein established a partisan movement there immediately after the Anschluss. Recruitment was effected as he drove his engine up and down the Brenner Pass when he was able to persuade war-weary troops to join his private army in Ötztal. So successful was this "Maquis" that the Gestapo placed a price of £3,500 on his head. The Sauerwein army captured four German generals, of which two were SS, and disarmed several German units. In May 1945 they made contact with the 44th US Infantry Division and led them into Tirol. After liberation was declared on 8th May, Sauerwein quietly returned to his engine.

Another mission was carried out on 2nd April by one of Major Szokoll's men, Sergeant Ferdinand Kaes, who bluffed his way through the German battle lines during the siege of Vienna to reach Marshal Tolbukhin's headquarters at Hoch-Wölkersdorf. There he presented valuable intelligence information to the Russian Front Commander regarding the location of German units including two crack SS divisions recently moved into position to defend the capital. The plan offered by Kaes, and accepted by the Russian Commander, was to outflank these units and attack Vienna from its soft western flank. In addition, and at a given signal, the entire resistance underground in Vienna would rise in revolt. The action duly started, as arranged, at dawn on 6th April but like many resistance engagements the leadership had been infiltrated and the plan disclosed secretly to the Gauleiter of Vienna, Baldur von Schirach. Although a partial success could be claimed, Major Biedermann was arrested and together with Captain Huth and Lieutenant Rashke hanged publicly in the suburb of Floridsdorf on 8th April. A few days later the siege ended and the red-white-red flag of Austria was finally struck from the spire of Stefanskirche. Sergeant Kaes escaped capture and, after the war, became Major of Gendarmerie in Vienna.

The above instances might not be regarded as constituting major examples of active resistance. Nevertheless they were carried out by patriots under the enormous risk, if caught, of being executed by the Gestapo without trial.

The Yugoslavs on the other hand claimed, with justification, that Slovene Carinthia was the only province of the Greater German Reich which offered armed resistance to the Nazis. In proportion to their numbers the Partisan Movement claimed that Carinthian Slovenes made an important contribution to the Allied struggle. Their repeated attacks against important lines of communication running across

Carinthia hindered the movement of troops and war material and tied down large units of the German army. The partisans also liberated many Allied prisoners of war and claimed that 12 per cent of the partisan detachments were made up of soldiers of various Allied countries whom they had freed from the Germans.

So effective was the Partisan Movement that in a speech in Klagenfurt on 10th July 1942, Maier-Kaibitsch, a dedicated Austrian Nazi, announced the "total extermination" of Slovenes in Carinthia and Upper Carniola for taking part in resistance activities. The Partisan Movement developed so successfully in Carinthia that the British sent in an Allied Military Mission to Slovenia. Until this occasion SOE had achieved virtually nothing on Austrian soil. One SOE member, Hesketh-Pritchard, was instructed by Allied Headquarters at Caserta, in late summer 1944, to help mobilise resistance in Carinthia. The possibility of the Allied armies reaching Vienna by Christmas that year was seriously considered. A specially designed folding boat to enable a crossing of the Drau was dropped by parachute. It is reported that more than 80 partisans joined Hesketh-Pritchard in making a successful crossing of the river and reaching the area of Saualpe north of Klagenfurt. Unfortunately the weather turned against him and supply drops could not be made. With little food and suffering intense cold in a hostile countryside he sent his last radio message on 3rd December requesting immediate food and reinforcements. From then on there was silence and Hesketh-Pritchard disappeared. His body was never found.

Other organisations accredited to the partisans were also involved in Slovenia with the objectives of arranging air-drop supplies of food, clothing and weapons for the partisans, organising sabotage to road and rail communications and industrial targets, gathering intelligence on enemy strength, locations and movements, and organising with the partisans escape routes for prisoners-of-war and refugees. These operations were carried out mainly in Slovene territory south of the Karawanken but on some occasions, for operational reasons, it was necessary for some units to cross northwards into Carinthia.

One officer involved in this way, Major J. C. Lambie, had been dropped into Macedonia at the beginning of 1944 and operated there until the German withdrawal from that area in late autumn. He was then re-infiltrated into Slovenia to liaise with the Partisan 9th Corps and recalls a typical crossing of the Karawanken into Carinthia.

Arms and ammunition containers being dropped by parachute from RAF Liberators and Wellingtons on a dropping zone north of Cerkno in Slovenia, 18th February 1945. 97 planes were sucessful and all stores recovered for Tito's partisans in Slovenia and Carinthia.

Apart from the Germans and the mountains, river crossings were always dangerous, especially in the winter conditions prevailing at that time. Many of the rivers, the Drau (Drava) for example, were wide, deep and fast flowing. Bridges were guarded and sections where it might have been possible to cross by boat or by wading were patrolled. In those conditions a bridge crossing was the only answer – the busier the bridge the better – but occasionally it was necessary to cover the usual British battledress with civilian clothing which could be discarded if capture seemed imminent. The road and rail links from Villach south to Italy were part of the principal escape routes for the Germans retreating from Italy and were therefore a target both for the partisans and the RAF – on occasions we could give information by radio direct to the RAF planes and guided them to targets. Supply drops were arranged by radio contact with Bari, and although these were made in Slovene territory, caches of equipment essential to the missions were spread out over a wide area for both security and convenience – many were never used and I wouldn't be surprised if some of those hidden in the mountains are still quite intact. Batteries were one of the essential items for maintaining our radio networks and if these were run down or had to be abandoned because of enemy action it became necessary to buy others locally – at a price, of course, and paid in gold Napoleons!

In the last few months of the war, with the Germans now in full retreat and desperate to secure their principal supply lines and communications through Slovenia, a great effort was made by them to clear the partisans from the area south of the Karawanken. In one of these "reactions" the partisan unit with Lambie was ambushed on 1st April 1945 and in the ensuing skirmish Lambie was wounded in the legs and left on the ground high in the mountains. He was picked up several hours later by a unit of the 10th SS Division. After medical attention on the spot, he was taken south to Idrija where he was in hospital for 3 days and subsequently survived a bombing and rocket raid on the town. He was then handed over to the Gestapo who took him to their H.Q. in Trieste for questioning.

Luckily, with the end of the war in sight, this involved little physical hardship, although he had to witness the hanging of four "Partisan Terrorists" and was told daily that in time he would be shot either as a spy or as a "terrorist". Two weeks later, however, the Gestapo arranged for him to be sent back under guard to Austria, presumably, he thought at the time, to a concentration camp. The journey took him by rail through Villach and up the Drau Valley where the line had been attacked on many occasions by the RAF. One main viaduct had been so badly damaged that the train was unable to cross. Lambie had to be carried over by his two guards – all this in darkness, driving snow and high wind. He remembers glancing through the gaping holes in the track and seeing the river far below and thinking that his captors could quite easily have dropped him into the swirling waters of the Drau, and another agent would have vanished. This did not happen, however, and today Lambie still praises the compassion and help afforded by his guards and indeed by all those who had captured him.

Lambie was eventually taken, not to a concentration camp – Dachau and Mauthausen were not far away – but to Stalag XVIIIB in Altenmarkt in Pongau, which at that time held prisoners of many nationalities – Russian (who were segregated from all others), British, American, French, Belgian, Dutch, Polish, Australian and, although a Stalag, had many of commissioned rank. He found himself to be the S.B.O. (Senior British Officer) and eventually the Senior Allied Officer. In theory, he was responsible for internal discipline throughout the camp. As his wounds prevented him from walking, the Commandant took him round the camp for daily inspection in his open car, an unusual procedure which was greeted with great cheering each day.

An unusual feature of this camp was the segregation of a group of the "Prominente" from Oflag IVC, Colditz, which had been liberated by the American 69th Infantry Division and 9th Armoured Division on 15/16th April. These included the Lord Lascelles, Captain the Master of Elphinstone, John Winant and the Polish General Bor. It was thought that such a group could be used as hostages in the event of a last ditch stand by the Germans.

Lambie, however, did not have long to wait in Stalag XVIIIB. He recalls:

After the Armistice was signed it was known that the nearest units of the American 7th Army were still 70-80 miles away. The German guards had given up their arms and were taken off the camp perimeter and discipline in the camp became difficult to control. There were still some dedicated SS units in the vicinity resisting surrender and all with itchy trigger fingers, and I felt it best to restrict movement from the camp – not easy and not very successful when dealing with troops some of whom had been prisoners for 4 years. I decided to send two American Lieutenants (O'Brien and Weeden) to try to make contact with the American advance troops, explain the position to them and ask for immediate help. It was a difficult and dangerous mission but they succeeded and two days later units of the 101st Airborne Division reached the camp and took control.

During the Second World War over 3,500 partisans fought in Carinthia of which 80 per cent were Slovene Carinthians. The first units were formed in September 1942, and in the Spring of 1943 the first Slovene Carinthian Partisans battalion was formed. Later a few Austrian battalions joined the struggle.

Because the relief of the country did not permit the operation of large companies, the partisans were obliged to operate in small units for sabotage purposes. These units claimed to have destroyed 67 lorries, 54 bridges, 26 trains, 53 locomotives, 219 railway cars, 3 railway stations, 1 aeroplane, 7 saw mills and 3 mines. This sabotage extended in an area from the Italian-Austrian border near Tarvisio in the west to Styria in the east and St Paul in the north but was mainly concentrated around Unterdrauburg (Dravograd) and Marburg (Maribor). These units also claimed to have carried out over 600 military engagements against the enemy between 1942 and the end of the war, the enemy suffering some 9,000 casualties killed, wounded or taken prisoner. The Partisans reported losing over one thousand killed in action, 710 wounded and 317 taken prisoner or declared missing. Some 150 enemy garrisons were said to be in Carinthia during this period.

A major retaliatory offensive against the partisans was undertaken by the Germans in May 1944. According to Yugoslav reports, the offensive starting point was a line Villach-Klagenfurt-Völkermarkt in a direction north-south. German units taking part were the 18th Landesschutzregiment, 112th Ersatzartillerieregiment, 134th Gebirgsjägerregiment, 13th SS Polizeiregiment, 137th, 138th and 139th Ersatzgebirgsjägerregiment, Gendarme stations and SA units.

Another major offensive was launched during the winter of 1944/45 and although the partisans sustained heavy losses in these offensives, both failed.

> *In Villach during the last year of the war I often heard in the distance the sound of gun-fire of partisan engagements with the Wehrmacht right across the Karawanken. It was frightening especially when the sky would be lit up like "Wetterleuchten" (lightning) from the battles. The situation was often confused by Allied bombing raids, the RAF by day, the Americans by night. A warning of the night raids was usually announced on the radio. The Americans would leave their base (initially Malta and later Bari) punctually at 8 pm which gave us sufficient time to pack our overnight case ready for another night in the shelter. Sometimes it was difficult to distinguish partisan attacks from bombing raids and sometimes both erupted together. These experiences still haunt me today.*
>
> *However, the war did not stop our regular school skiing outings. These were usually to the 7000 feet Dobratsch mountain near Villach. During the last two winters of the war it was becoming dangerous on the mountain because of low flying RAF planes which would come down so low that we could see the pilot's face quite clearly. Our teacher instructed us to carry a white sheet in our rucksack on these outings so that as soon as we heard enemy planes approaching we were to fall on the snow and cover ourselves with the sheets. Otherwise it was possible that we may have been wrongly identified as German or Austrian troops on manoeuvres.*

The effect of partisan resistance resulted in large areas of Carinthia being under their control during the latter years of the war. Committees of the Liberation Movement, supported politically by the Soviet Union sprang up in many towns and villages throughout Slovene Carinthia. According to Yugoslav claims, there were nearly one hundred of these Committees functioning before the end of the war. The function of the Committees was to infiltrate institutions and factories, carry out intelligence and perform sabotage tasks.

The epic struggle of Tito's Partisans in Yugoslavia during the Second World War is well known in the west and is now history. The exploits of the Slovene Carinthians however are less well known possibly because both the Allies and Austria preferred not to publicise them after the war for political reasons. Nevertheless they formed an important part of Yugoslavia's titanic struggle against the Nazi enemy.

In addition to active resistance to the Nazi regime inside Austria, passive resistance sprung up outside the country particularly in Britain and the United States. In Britain the Free Austria Movement had a wartime membership of some 7,000 and a world membership of 25,000. Its central office was in London at 124 Westbourne Terrace and social functions and lectures were held up and down the country. The organisation was mainly composed of Jewish exiles and there was some evidence that it had Communist sympathies. The Free Austria Movement, however, had many well-known personalities in Britain and became very strong during the last winter of the war in preparation for the Liberation. There were additional offices in Eton Avenue and Seven Sisters Road in London, and area offices in Glasgow, Manchester, Birmingham, Oxford, Cambridge and Newcastle. The movement had some liaison with the 'Young Austrians in Great Britain" and the German Democratic Union in London with offices at 29 Dorset Square. The Anglo-Austrian Society, an independent body, was founded in London in 1944 by British friends of Austria and Austrians in exile in the United Kingdom. "to assist in the re-establishment of a free and independent democratic Austria and to promote friendship between the peoples of Great Britain and Austria".

The Habsburg brothers too were also playing their part during the war while in exile in Britain and the United States.

The last Habsburg emperor, Charles, had five sons, Otto, Felix, Karl Ludwig, Robert and Rudolf and all of them were active during the war. Otto was the Heir or "Crown Prince" who normally organised their operations from the United States. Churchill, and surprisingly Roosevelt too admired them, much to Eden's embarrassment. Churchill wrote:

> *It seemed unlucky that the Habsburgs, having produced so many regrettable specimens in the past, should at last have turned out these admirable young brothers, of which any dynasty may be proud.*

Schuschnigg too had leanings towards the Habsburgs and in February 1938, when the Anschluss seemed imminent, Otto sent a letter to the Austrian Chancellor by special messenger from Belgium imploring him as a former officer of the Austrian Army to appoint him, Otto, to the post of Chancellor if such a step would save Austria.

During the critical years for Austria of 1936-38, the monarchy had a strong following in many parts of the country. They were fervently anti-Nazi and everything that Hitler stood for was anathema to them and by the end of 1936, some 1,456 Austrian municipalities had made Archduke Otto their "honorary citizen".

However any attempt to restore the Habsburg monarchy in Austria before the war would inevitably have led to military occupation by Hitler. Schuschnigg was so informed of this by Hermann Göring and, by the political leaders in Belgrade, Prague and Bucharest.

Churchill had a secret meeting with Otto in 1943 in Quebec. Later Otto would say that they differed on only one point: Otto wanted Croatia to be part of a central European federation but Churchill wanted to restore Yugoslavia to its 1938 frontiers. Otto thought the British were blind to the Soviet danger and that only Churchill saw it. Churchill told Eden of the conversation and suggested that one of the greatest mistakes of the First World War was "the destruction by ignorant hands of the Austro-Hungarian Empire".

Churchill had lunch with Otto in Quebec the following year when Otto told him that he had just given Roosevelt a letter proposing that he, Otto, should go in secret to the Swiss-French border and work with a former Hungarian diplomat to bring the Hungarian Government to terms with the Western Allies. The aim was to save Hungary from Communist domination and, if a general uprising in Austria could be brought about at the same time, he would request Churchill to supply the necessary arms "for my people".

But by March 1945 the Soviet Union had occupied Hungary. Otto still had hopes for Austria, however, and wrote to Churchill from Paris requesting arms, explosives, radio equipment and money for resistance organisations in Austria. He reported that he and his brothers were trying unsuccessfully to join his people's struggle in Austria.

The Foreign Office however was unsympathetic to Otto's overtures and no doubt for very good reasons. There was little chance of a monarchist revival in Austria and even if there was her neighbours would never permit it.

However Otto proceeded to sow the seeds of monarchy wherever and whenever possible. When he turned up in Brussels to the consternation of the Belgium Prince Regent and the British Ambassador, His Excellency notified the Foreign Office. In response Churchill telegraphed his Ambassador.

> *The principle of constitutional monarchy, provided it is based on the will of the people, is not – oddly enough – abhorrent to the British mind. Personally, having lived through all these European disturbances and studied carefully their causes, I am of the opinion that if the Allies at the peace table at Versailles had not imagined that the sweeping away of the long established dynasties was a form of progress —— there would have been no Hitler —— This is a personal view but perhaps you would like to meditate upon it.*

In August 1945 a few months after the British occupied Carinthia, Archduke Robert, together with his brother Archduke Felix, arrived incognito in Klagenfurt. They had travelled in uniform posing as French Lieutenants with the pseudonyms of Weber and Lamprecht. They held well attended meetings of the Peoples Party both in Klagenfurt on the 9th of August, and also had meetings in Villach and Graz. They spoke with monarchists and sympathisers and slipped out of Carinthia by way of Lienz to Salzburg and Tirol and later Vorarlberg in which places they were reported to have held similar meetings.

In maintaining an active interest in the situation in the three occupied zones of Austria (there was no way they would risk entering the Soviet Zone), Archduke Robert reported to the Foreign Office in July 1945.

> *I left out the part concerning the British Zone in Austria because I felt that these you know much more than I do. Anyway what was said was most flattering on your people's ability of organising and most grateful about your attitude towards the claim put forward by Tito on Carinthia.*

In his report on the U.S. Zone however he was not so complimentary and suggested that the US 7th Army seemed not to have been "fully prepared to take over the occupation of Austria" and had "committed many errors" which apparently had an upsetting effect on the most ardent friends of the Allies. He continued:

> *The American troops consider the population as Germans and Nazis — and the officers always stress the fact that they have come as victors.*
>
> *[A] great number of Nazis are still free and many of them have been and are employed by the American authorities in their administration. These Nazis accuse the Austrian patriots to the American authorities as Nazis. It is thus that many people who have been either in concentration camps or have taken an active part in the resistance are regarded with grave suspicion by the American authorities.*
>
> *The Americans, although full of the very best intentions, are making themselves most unpopular and are exasperated by the opposition they find from a population infuriated by the support the Americans are giving, without knowing it, to the Nazis.*
>
> *The Americans having only very few officers speaking the native language, and using many former Nazis as interpreters, are creating a chaos of which only the Nazis can profit. The superior officers are sending to Washington reports on the situation in Austria describing the lack of pro-Allied feelings of the Austrian population without realising that they themselves are the cause of these feelings. Thus the situation is rapidly deteriorating and if Washington is not going to change the methods used in Austria a wonderful occasion will be missed and a very ugly xenophobia might develop.*

Archduke concluded his report:

> *In the whole of Austria there is a great need for the establishment of free newspapers. All Nazis have not yet*

been rounded up and they are spreading rumours which create a great deal of unrest. They say that the whole of Austria will be handed over to the Russians by the Allies, that inflation is created artificially by the Allies and so on.

In this way they hope, together with the communists, to render collaboration between the Allies and the population impossible. A free and well run press could be used to dissipate all those rumours and work for the collaboration between the Allies and the Austrians. The radio stations of Vorarlberg, Innsbruck, Linz, Klagenfurt and eventually Graz could also be used for this purpose.

In the last year of the war Archduke Robert wrote to the Prime Minister from his address in London in an endeavour to join the RAF and to form an Austrian combatant unit:

Dear Mr Prime Minister,

A few days ago Sir George Franckenstein (former Austrian Ambassador to Britain) handed to you a resumé of a memorandum in which he suggested that the loyal Austrian prisoners of war should be allowed to form a combatant unit for the liberation of my dear country from the oppression of their century long enemy. If this suggestion could be accepted every true Austrian patriot would, I am sure, throw all his energy into the fight and gladly sacrifice his life in our common struggle.

I have devoted my life since the beginning of this war to further every means at my disposal the interest of the Allied nations and the great cause of democracy in Austria. It has always been my ardent desire to play an active part in this war and to strike a blow in the defence of freedom and justice for which principles Great Britain has heroically taken up the fight and the ultimate liberty of my beloved homeland.

For this reason I have endeavoured to join the RAF and later the Parachute Corps but both times I have been unsuccessful. The unfortunate disbanding of the Austrian

Battalion in the U.S. Army deprived me of that service also. My request now my dear Mr Prime Minister is that should you and your cabinet see fit to permit the formation of an Austrian force within the framework of His Britannic Majesty's Army, that I may be accepted for service with this force. My one object in this war is that I may serve our great common cause in some way that may be of use to the Allies, and especially Great Britain, and for the salvation and the re-establishment of my oppressed and tortured country.

Yours sincerely,

Robert of Austria

There were in fact about one thousand Austrians in the British Army almost all of them in the Pioneer Corps. Individual Austrians with suitable qualifications and subject to a security check were permitted to volunteer for service in almost any unit including Combatant units of the British Armed Forces, but there was no separate Austrian unit which Archduke Robert was proposing to the Prime Minister. The potential numbers for such a unit would have been about ten thousand, being mostly prisoners of war in Britain and France. The advantages of such a policy might have been to encourage Austrian prisoners of war to desert from the German Army and raise national feeling in Austria. The danger, however, was that such a policy might have led to trouble with Germans in P.O.W. camps who might accuse the British of compelling Austrians (who they considered as German nationals) to fight against Germany. In addition any such Austrians captured in the field could have expected severe punishment from the Nazis. Nevertheless the War Office continued their policy of recruiting Austrian P.O.W.'s into combatant units of the British Armed Forces until the end of the war.

If the Habsburgs saw the war as an opportunity to reinstate the dynasty in Austria the chance came immediately after the war when the establishment of an Alpine Federal State with the Habsburgs at its head was seriously proposed. On the 6th December 1945, a movement was launched to set up a breakaway State from Austria and Southern Germany with a population of more than 20 million. It was perhaps no coincidence that the idea emanated from Bregenz in the French Zone of occupation. The French were very sympathetic at the time to the

Habsburg cause. The movement became know as the "Action Committee of the Alpine democratic Union" and was led by prominent Austrian provincial leaders. There seems little doubt that the French encouraged the Action Committee and most of its leaders occupied high posts under the French. The frontiers visualised extended from the Western border of Southern Czechoslovakia to the Tirol and from Vienna to the Rhine and Neckar. Lower and Upper Bavaria with the cities of Munich, Regensburg and Augsburg and the Province of Swabia, Würthenberg and Baden would also be incorporated. The new State would cover some 195,000 square miles and federated on Swiss lines with the Provinces enjoying regional autonomy.

It will be recalled that a similar situation arose after the First World War when unofficial plebiscites held in Tirol and Salzburg resulted in large majorities for cession to Bavaria.

Archduke Otto's stock had apparently risen in Vorarlberg and Tirol where the People's Party swept the polls in the general election of November 1945. However, the Bavarian royalists were reluctant to support the Habsburgs and see them on the throne, and in time the movement fizzled out.

This was the nearest Archduke Otto came to restoring the monarchy in Austria. For him there would never be another chance.

6

THE FALL OF VIENNA

Soviet troops of the Third Ukrainian Front invaded Austria from the Hungarian town of Koeszeg on 29th March 1945 and towns and villages began falling to the Russians all over eastern Austria. The Western Allies, however, were at this time a long way from Austria. The U.S. Sixth Army were just expanding their River Main bridgehead, and the 12th Armoured Division were moving on Würzburg. The French First Army were crossing the Rhine at Speyer and Germensheim. On the Italian front the British Eighth Army were approaching Lake Comacchio, and the U.S. Fifth Army were moving on Bologna. Churchill's plan to scrap the invasion of the South of France (Anvil) and instead push up the Sava Valley through the Ljubljana Gap, if it had been agreed, may well have changed the whole situation in eastern Europe. Certainly the plan may have ensured that the Western Allies would take Vienna before the Russians and prevent great suffering in that unfortunate City. As it was, the battle for Vienna was long and bloody and lasted for eight days from 6th to 13th April. When it was over much of the City lay in ruins.

Out of a total of 59,000 houses, 2,000 were totally destroyed, nearly 5,000 partially destroyed, and over 5,000 seriously damaged.

The Red Army were at first greeted by the population as liberators but in a very short time this soon changed to fear and mistrust by their behaviour.

It is said that during the early days Russian troops entered houses on the pretext of searching for weapons and took whatever they pleased. Women and children were driven to remain in hiding for days on end. Notices were pinned on house doors stating in both Russian and German, "this house has been searched". According to statistics kept by the Public Health Authorities some 87,000 women were raped during the first three weeks of the Russian occupation.

There were understandably mitigating circumstances for the Russians' behaviour in Austria in the early months after the end of the Second World War. Their revenge for the suffering of their own people during the war knew no bounds. Although they were at war for only 49 months compared to Britain's 71 months (America was at war for 44 months), they had lost no less than 20 million of their people. One and a half million of these were killed during the siege of Leningrad which lasted for 900 days, from September 1941 until January 1944, when three million people were trapped inside the city. One million of these people lie today in a common grave in the Piskarevsky Cemetery which has become a national shrine. By the end of the war one-quarter of all Soviet property had been destroyed including 17,000 towns, 70,000 villages, 31,000 factories and 84,000 schools. Twenty-five million people were homeless, and forced to live in unhealthy huts, cellars or dug-out holes in the ground. In addition five million people were considered as displaced persons including 600,000 children. By the end of the war six million new homes would be required. Under such infliction in war the desire for vengeance was understandably predominant.

Viennese citizens mourned at the graves of those who died during the siege. The Germans had taken all able bodied men and motor transport; the dead were left lying lightly covered with earth. The photograph shows British troops using bulldozers to fill in the open massed graves. In the background a few people can be seen searching for the graves of their lost loved ones (17th August 1945).

Meanwhile, many thousands of the Viennese population lived under appalling conditions with a single suit of clothes and without domestic equipment or having to share this with other families. Tens of thousands of children were scattered throughout camps in Germany and Austria about which no information was available. Parents waited for months on end for news of children aged 10 - 14 years. Others not more than 16 years of age made their way back from service in the Wehrmacht and the Volkssturm (Home Guard) and abandoned themselves to the most dubious amusements such as assisting in dance halls. It was quite a common occurrence for girls to give themselves over to prostitution to earn a living.

A British food train arrives in Vienna. Vienna in the summer of 1945 was a city of misery, suffering and death. The food shortage reached catastrophic levels and supplies had to be rushed in from Britain and the United States to avoid a serious famine (17th August 1945).

Deterioration was seen everywhere. The health situation in June 1945 was critical. Because many doctors left Vienna the clinics for skin diseases and sex ailments were unable to cope with the number of cases. In the circumstances the Austrian health authorities worked wonders, despite the fact that they were denied the assistance of the International Red Cross, which the Russians did not recognise. Water could only be drunk after boiling owing to dysentry and typhus epidemics in the city. Serums and even the most rudimentory medicines were lacking to combat disease and the death rate during the first few months of "liberation" was high. Owing to the scarcity of anaesthetics even the most urgent operations could not be carried out. Epidemics raged in the 2nd and 20th districts especially and these districts were declared in quarantine and sealed off. All military hospitals were filled with civilians even although there was insufficient beds to accommodate all the inmates.

There were many stories which went around Vienna during this period. It was widely reported, for instance, that Russian troops used the bath or wash-basin as toilets in their requisitioned apartments and even stripped fittings from houses and buildings under the Russians' interpretation of their right to rehabilitate their own war damaged cities with material from cities they captured.

In the 13th district it was reported that a Russian general had all the women and girls within reach collected in the church square and paraded naked. He then chose for himself the most attractive. Russian soldiers forced girls from neighbouring houses at pistol point to accompany them to places of entertainment, if there were not enough there. The Red Army women soldiers did the same with men, if they found none to dance with. There were also stories told of Soviet women soldiers raping men at pistol point. Cafés and bars were open from noon to 10 pm (curfew time) and did active business.

Surprisingly, the Russians gave priority for theatres, cinemas, dance-halls and cafés to be opened again. But all these activities were under strict Russian control, and Russian soldiers made their wishes known in most places of amusement at the point of the pistol. Shops opened again but for the most part had nothing in them because of looting by the soldiers.

The deliveries of food by the Red Army at the beginning of June averted the danger of famine, but went only half-way to meeting the more urgent needs. Before that, food supplies had dwindled to nothing. Rations became available from time to time and food queues diminished. Fresh milk (¹/₈ litre per day) appeared for children up to the age of three but nothing for mothers or expectant mothers nor any provision for older children. The meat was partially taken out in horseflesh. Fruit and vegetables were virtually unobtainable for many months. Bread, which in Vienna was always regarded as of the highest quality, was now only slightly better than during the last days of the Nazi occupation. During the weekends people in the suburbs queued to barter their last possessions for foodstuffs from the country. The cost of a pound of butter in Vienna was as much as 500 marks and a pound of cooking fat 1,000 marks.

The transport situation in the first few months of liberation was chaotic. The Russians and the Nazis between them removed all vehicles they could get their hands on. Bicycles too were requisitioned by Red Army troops and even hospital cases had to be transported by hand-cart. The Soviet authorities did, however, return on loan at the beginning of May some 200 lorries, otherwise all transport was commandeered for Russian needs and very few used to bring in food from the countryside. The tramway lines, however, were very soon repaired but trains ran only as far as Graz in the south and then only at the whim of the Russian officer in charge. People were free to travel in the Russian Zone without permits but were liable to be summarily impressed for labour, sometimes for a day and sometimes for a whole week without warning for forced labour as far as Bratislava.

Only comparitively few Nazis were arrested initially and the Nazis denounced members of the resistance movement, as they did later in other zones of occupation, in order to procure alibis for themselves. One active member of the resistance was thus denounced and shot before any explanation could be made.

The monarchists were being rounded up and according to second-hand reports were being imprisoned. Their names were known to the Russians owing to the prominent part they played in the resistance.

The General Headquarters of the 05 resistance Organization at 13 Herrengasse was seized by the Russian secret police (GPU) and its staff arrested. Some were liquidated, others deported, according to reports, in spite of the fact that members of the Provisional Government belonged to the organization. The Minister for Social Welfare was literally picked up one day in the street for forced labour, his credentials being ignored. Nazis were set to work in labour gangs clearing the rubble from Vienna's streets but most workers were reported to be engaged in dismantling factories and machines could be seen all day long on their way to the East via the Favoriten railway station. Many workmen were apparently moved with their machines.

It was said that few young men were left in Vienna and those who survived the war were either in Soviet prison camps or Nazis in jail.

All businesses and buildings that passed into the hands of the Nazis since the Anschluss were confiscated. The Russians re-introduced newspapers, the "New Austria" under Russian censorship and "Osterreichischer Zeiting" issued by the Red Army in both Russian and German. The Vienna radio was also under Russian censorship.

Austria had provided the Russians with their first prolonged mass contact with the west. After the early post-war months, the Russian soldiers' conduct improved out of all recognition. Most of the problems were claimed to have been caused by front-line troops getting drunk for many days in glorious celebration of an historic victory after having fought every step of the way from Stalingrad to Vienna. However, many stories about the Red Army's conduct after liberation had been greatly exaggerated. People would spread stories around Vienna about some terrible thing happening to their friends but never to themselves. Many among the poor had nothing against the Red Army, except their continued presence – but this applied to all the Allies.

The average Russian, however, did not believe that the Austrians had sufficiently broken with "their tainted past" and declared that thousands of Austrians in German uniforms were in the Wehrmacht vanguard at the siege of Stalingrad. After the November 1945 Austrian elections, when the Communists failed badly, the Russians became more dogged against the Austrians and showed more interest in that part of the Moscow Declaration which made Austria's liberation dependent on the degree of effort she exerted to achieve it herself. Like the Yugoslavs, they considered that Austrians were not victims of Hitler's Anschluss but perpetrators of it. The two characters mixed badly, "the Russians clumsy and herculean, the Austrians negative and ultra-civilized".

The Russians also accused the Austrian Government for their lackadaisical approach to denazification. Only two important war trials had taken place in the twelve months after the war and several accused had been waiting in prisons for many months and others were still at large. On the other hand the Austrians accused the Russians of developing their objections into an elaborate case of turning their zone into an eastern satellite, and eventual partition of the Country, as they had done in Germany with their "eastern zone".

A correspondent of *The Times*, however, spent a week in the spring of 1946 on an unconducted tour of the Russian Zone in Lower Austria and Burgenland. Relations between the Austrians and Russians he found to be good. The fields of vines were all being cultivated except those in the vicinity of the "Ost Wall" which the Germans tried to build with 80,000 foreign forced labour to stem the Russian advance. In Wiener Neustadt, formerly a large industrial area the population before the war of 45,000 had dropped to 27,000. Sixty per cent of the houses were damaged by British and American bombing and Russian artillery. The Russian troops lived in barracks and required a pass to visit the town. The Bürgermeister confirmed to the correspondent that relations with the Russians were good and that they had done much to help the people.

The Russian officers with whom I spoke gave the impression of being extremely hard-working and intelligent men. They went to great pains to arrange that I saw on my own all I wished to see and were willing to discuss frankly any criticisms.

The Russian troops in Mauthausen were billeted in the former concentration camp and a large picture of Stalin looked across the parade ground. Twenty Russian soldiers slept in a room where there were once 1,500 prisoners. *The Times* correspondent was shown the crematorium, gas chambers and execution rooms by the Soviet Commandant. In the little cemetery under the walls of the camp were hundreds of crosses marking the graves of victims nearly all with the word "Unknown" written on them. It was to Mauthausen that fifty-four SOE officers were sent for their part in the Englandspiel affair in Holland in 1942/43. Unknown to SOE in London everyone of these fifty-four agents dropped into Holland was known to the Germans and all were captured on landing. Half of the number died in Mauthausen serving hard labour in the infamous quarry. The remainder were exterminated. Only five survived the war. In the company of Russian journalists the correspondent visited two Habsburg castles and was shown round by the Archduke and his wife. One castle belonged to the Duke of Hohenburg, son of the Archduke Franz Ferdinand, whose assassination at Sarajevo led to the First World War. The Duke spent a long time with his brother in Dachau and was elected Bürgermeister of the village with the approval of the Russians. The other castle belonged to a grandson of Emperor Franz Josef and the correspondent was taken through the castle by the Archduke where, in the Great Hall, Marshal Tolbukhin and General Patton held a banquet to celebrate the meeting of the two armies in Austria.

The Archduke confirmed that the Russian soldiers had done no damage to the castle or its interior. There were large numbers of Russian troops stationed in the nearby towns of Melk and Amstetten. The interest of Russians in history and historical monuments became evident in Melk whose famous abbey had been used by the Nazis as a school for Hitler Youth. When the Russians arrived they at once mounted a permanent guard, and the Monks confirmed that no damage had been done. Melk was the centre of the last fighting of the war and the custodian of the abbey first knew that the Nazis had been driven out when he heard the abbey organ being played and went in to find a Russian soldier seated at the keys.

In addition to the damage from street fighting, Vienna suffered severe damage from the Allied bombing although it is perhaps fair to say that it escaped the devastation of some English and German cities such as Coventry, Hamburg, Cologne and Dresden. Since the bomber flights had to be carried out from bases beyond the Alps, this limited the size of both the bombs and the scale of the raids. Most of the objects of art however were either evacuated or stored in Vienna's deep cellars and so escaped damage or destruction. Of Vienna's museums the Kunsthistorisches Museum received four direct hits by bombs and The Albertina was also severely bombed, but the Technical Museum suffered only some roof damage and broken windows.

Damage to Vienna's great architectural buildings, however, disfigured the inner city for many years. The most serious of all, and most deeply felt by the Viennese, was the damage done to St Stephen's Cathedral (Stephanskirche), Austria's greatest Gothic monument (circa 1300) which was burnt during the fighting between the attacking Russians and the defending Germans on 12th April. Apparently the fire was caused by blazing fragments from an adjacent carpet warehouse being carried by wind across the street and setting fire to some scaffolding. The fire then spread to the roof through holes in the tiles caused by the shelling. The roof, supported by 3,000 wooden beams, burnt from end to end and two-thirds of the choir vaulting fell in, although the vaulting of the nave was hardly damaged. All the furniture in the choir was lost as well as the organ and windows of the nave. Remarkably the three towers and the spire (Alte Stefferl) were left standing with only minor damage to the stonework. The great 20 ton bell (the Great Pummerin) in the tower cast from 200 Turkish cannons fell and broke into pieces. The British began preserving the structure that remained soon after they entered Vienna but restoration was not effected until 1954 when the new Pummerin recast at St Florian was, amid rejoicing, transported through the country to Vienna and installed in the tower of this Cathedral dedicated to the patron saint of Vienna. The complete restoration which had cost some 20 million schillings was financed entirely by subscriptions and collections but was not fully completed until the organ was installed in 1960.

The damage to other Gothic structures was relatively minor but British help was given for urgent protective work to prevent further deterioration.

The Opera House, built in 1869, suffered severe damage in a bombing raid on 12th March when the interior and roof were completely destroyed. Of all the great buildings in Vienna the Opera House experienced the worst damage and full restoration took ten years to complete. Also seriously damaged were the imperial stables used for the Vienna Fair, Parliament House and the Burg Theatre whose interior was completely destroyed by fire and was not opened again until 1955. The Hofburg, the former Habsburg Imperial Palace, and the National Library emerged almost unscathed. The Liechtenstein Palace lost its roof and celebrated staircase and the Harkach Palace also suffered damage.

Beyond the inner city the worst bombed area was around the Sud Bahnhof including the Belvedere which received a direct hit. The famous caryatid staircase and the great marble salon were undamaged while the decorations of the beautiful gold room had been removed for safety. The forecourt, however, was in ruins and the baroque gardens were pitted with bomb craters. The Marmor Saal and the Gretschen Saal were severely damaged but the lovely entrance courtyard was untouched. The Schwarzenberg Palace begun in 1697 by Fischer von Erlach and completed in 1715 by his son received direct hits during the bombing and such was the damage that the building had to be almost rebuilt and restoration was not completed until ten years later.

One direct hit was scored on Schönbrunn Palace, begun under Emperor Leopold I in 1694 but not completed until 1749 under Maria-Theresa. The scale of the attack could be seen by the 300 or so bomb craters which peppered the grounds. The massive construction of the Palace with its 1,400 rooms saved it from extensive damage although a large hole was blown in the roof. The only serious loss, however, was one of three ceiling frescoes by Gughelm in the Great Gallery depicting ironically the "Glorification of War".

The paintings and tapestries which had been removed to distant depots for safety were brought back under British arrangements. The structural damage was repaired with British help and the park remained open and although one end of the Gloriette was in ruins, the famous view could still be enjoyed from the roof.

Soviet permission for the Western Allies to enter Vienna required a joint appeal from Churchill and Truman to Stalin. Churchill wrote to Stalin on 30th April:

> *It has been our understanding that the treatment of Austria, as of Germany, is a matter of common concern to the Four Powers who are to occupy and control these countries. We regard it as essential that British, American and French representatives should be allowed to proceed at once to Vienna in order to report on conditions there . . . We hope you will issue the necessary instructions to Marshal Tolbukhin in order that the Allied Mission may fly in at once from Italy.*

In a message to the Prime Minister on 18th May Marshal Stalin agreed.

On hearing subsequently of the proposals which the Chiefs of Staff and Foreign Office had in mind, Churchill was uneasy that the Mission might probe too deeply in Vienna and sent the following message to Eden on 1st June:

> *I presume this makes it clear that we are only discussing questions of accommodation in Vienna for our representatives and their staff, or does it mean that we are to fish around and find out all that is going on behind the "iron curtain"? If the latter, much as I should like to have it, it is rather more than I asked Stalin, or he conceded.*

The Military Mission, with General Winterton representing Britain, arrived in Vienna on 3rd June and although they received a cordial welcome from Marshal Tolbukhin, the Marshal insisted that they left again by 10th June. The Mission actually managed to delay their departure until 13th June when they reported back to their respective Governments. The arrival of the Allied Military Mission, however, was greeted with enthusiasm by the Viennese who feared that Russia might continue to control Vienna and the surrounding area indefinitely. Even then however they still wondered when the Western Powers were actually going to occupy the Capital for this was the foremost wish of all Viennese. The occupation zones were not finally confirmed until the first week in August when the Western Allies at last took up the Four Power occupation of Vienna.

Instead of the once gay city, the Western Allies found a city on the point of starvation. Food supplies were therefore given the utmost priority and were rushed in from the U.S. and British Zones to stave off immediate famine until such time as supplies could be organised on a more regular basis. Children and the elderly were most vulnerable and the infant mortality rate was as high as 1 in 4. In Europe as a whole at this time it was estimated that some 150 million people required immediate food aid to avoid famine and Vienna was at the tail end of this bread line. The daily ration fell as dangerously low as 800 calories while experts claimed that the minimum subsistence level was 1,550 calories (the British diet was 3,000 calories). Feeding Vienna was therefore on a day to day basis and to the annoyance of the British and Americans (French supplies were provided by the U.S.) the Russians were using food supplies from their zone to feed their massive army with surplus being transported to the Soviet satellites. The Soviet Zone normally produced 65 per cent of all Austria's agricultural products from an arable area of some 40,000 acres and therefore constituted the main supply to Vienna.

When UNRRA assumed responsibility for food distribution in Europe that organisation estimated that some 11 million tons of food was required urgently to avoid starvation in several countries. The United States supplied 44 per cent of this and Britain and the Commonwealth 40 per cent. In its first year of operation UNRRA spent $59 million on food supplies to Austria of which the United States' contribution was 73 per cent.

Emergencies continued to arise from time to time, however, due to delivery difficulties, world shortages, or drought conditions in Austria itself. One such emergency arose early in 1946 when the four Allied Armies had to supply 114 tons of food immediately to maintain the ration at 1,200 calories per day. Of this total the British were able to contribute nearly half and in addition diverted two food shiploads on the high seas to Austria, enough for two weeks supply.

In the summer of 1946 rations were necessarily drastically reduced in Austria. Talk of calorific value and quantity in grams was all rather vague to the average British housewife but the photograph shows just what her counterpart in Vienna got for a week's ration (14th June 1945).

The ration for the week commencing 14th June 1946, for example, was as follows:-

    2 oz egg powder
    1 oz fat
    3½ oz peas
    6½ oz potatoes
    2 oz oatmeal/porridge oats
    1¾ oz dried milk
    2¼ lb bread

It took some five years before it could be said that the food problem was solved in Austria. Even in 1948 the estimated cost of imported food to maintain a tolerable diet was $160 million.

Although Britain played a large part in food aid to Vienna and at a time of shortages at home, by far the largest contributor was the United States. This was recognised by the Austrian Government in 1948 when a public notice was printed on food packets which read:

60 per cent of your rations is a gift from the United States

The Allied Control machinery in Austria consisted of an Allied Council, an executive committee and staffs. The whole organisation was known as the Allied Commission for Austria. Their primary task was the complete separation of Austria from Germany. The council consisted of four military, or high, commissioners (from 1950 the Western Allies appointed their Ambassadors) who jointly exercised supreme authority in Austria. Each commissioner was also commander-in-chief of the forces of occupation of their respective Governments.

The administration of the City of Vienna operated under the direction of the Allied Council and its four commandants and jointly occupied by the four powers. The inner City was occupied by the armed forces of all four Powers, the districts of Leopoldstadt, Brigittenau, Floridsdorf, Wieden and Favoriten by the Soviet Union; the districts of Nebau, Josefstadt, Hernals, Alsergrund, Währing and Döbling by the United States; the districts of Mariahilf, Penzing, Fünfhaus, Rudolfsheim and Ottakring by France; the districts of Hietzing, Margareten, Meidling, Landstrasse and Semmering by the United Kingdom.

The functions of the Allied Commission for Austria were:

(a) to ensure the enforcement in Austria of the provisions of the Declaration regarding the defeat of Germany signed at Berlin on 5th June 1945.

(b) to achieve the separation of Austria from Germany.

(c) to secure the establishment, as soon as possible, of a central Austrian administration machine.

(d) to prepare the way for establishment of a freely elected Austrian Government.

(e) Meanwhile to provide for the administration of Austria to be carried on satisfactorily.

(f) to ensure the institution of a progressive long-term educational programme designed to eradicate all traces of Nazi ideology and to instil into Austrian youth democratic principles.

VIENNA : DISTRICTS OF OCCUPATION

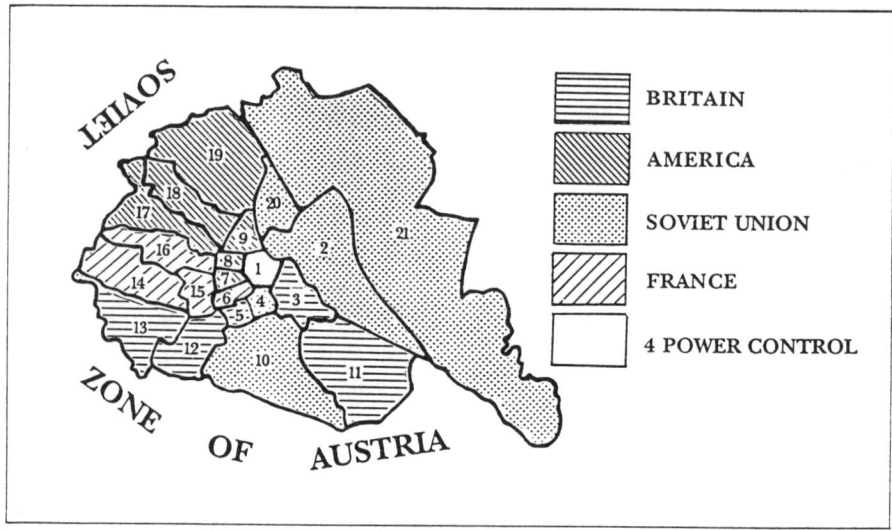

The changing of the Guard at Schönbrunn Palace, Vienna took place for the first time on the 6th August 1945 when the 2nd Battalian Lancashire Fusiliers took over from 2771 Sqn. RAF Regiment. The band of the 4th Hussars played during the ceremony.

The Austrian State Curator expressed the liveliest pleasure when he was informed that Schönbrunn was to be used as the British Headquarters in Austria. Every precaution was taken to avoid damage to the Palace and a member of the Fine Arts and Monuments Branch, who was an expert in such matters, was sent out from London with a reconnaisance party to advise on the treatment and use of the Palace and ensure that everything possible was done to protect the rooms from damage. In view of the possibility of accidental damage, however, the British decided not to use some of the more important State rooms. The Russians had occupied the Palace since they entered Vienna; Napoleon made it his headquarters in 1805; now it was General McCreery, British Military Commissioner and Commander-in-Chief, who took up residence in this historical edifice which had celebrated the birth of Emperor Franz Joseph in 1830 and mourned his death in 1916. The British occupied the Palace until 1948 when it was handed back to Austria. In making the announcement acting British High Commissioner, Major General Winterton, on behalf of General Galloway said that due to the reduction of British forces in Austria Britain had decided to hand back the Palace to the Austrian Government:

> *It has been a great privilege to have had the use of this lovely historic building. We have done our best to preserve and help restore the building from the ravages of war. I hope it will not be long before the Palace is completely restored to its former glory and to the full enjoyment of the Austrian people.*

7

BTA

BRITISH TROOPS IN AUSTRIA

During the ten years of their occupation of Austria, British troops were also to be found in practically all corners of the globe. The East writhed in turmoil of a continent in rebirth and independence in the wake of Western colonialisation had brought instability. Above all was the threat of an atomic war which could have destroyed civilisation. The agressor was Communism which dominated one-third of the world's people. The United States, Britain and France, the free world's principal member States were at odds over China, Spain, German rearmament and a United Europe. To reason in time to halt Communist aggression was the vital problem of the free world in the early fifties. A reign of terror swept China and it is believed that more than one million Chinese were killed for offences against the Communist Government during the first 20 months of its rule. This, if true, was a record of mass killings surpassed only in modern times by the bloody deeds of Hitler and Stalin. Also in the early fifties Tito was under threat from the Soviet Union and his answer reverberated round the world, "We will raise one and a half million men and fight to the death", to which Stalin replied: "I will lift my little finger and there will be no more Tito".

The situation was so serious that the United States Secretary of State Dean Acheson declared that an attack by Russia or her satellite armies upon Yugoslavia might well set off World War III.

The Korea conflict flared up on 25th June 1950 when the North Korean Army roared across the 38th parallel. Troops from 17 nations fought there and Britain sent some 22,000 men. In the first year of the conflict the Allies lost a quarter of a million men and the Communists over a million.

In 1951 some 4,000 front-line troops of the British 29th Brigade suffered 25 per cent casualties in less than three days of heroic battle. The 1st Battalion of the Gloucestershire Regiment alone lost an estimated 560 of its 600 man complement.

In this fight against the Red aggression the United States had to lead the free world. Ravaged by the Second World War the other free nations lacked the necessary military and economic strength. French troops, however, were in Indo-China fighting the Communist forces of Ho Chi Minh and Britain was forced to keep an army of some 200,000 men overseas on guard against Communism in Malaya, the Middle East and other outposts.

Austria by comparison by 1948 was a relatively quiet posting for British troops and although Britain had 65,000 men in the British Zone at the end of 1945 (the US and France had 47,000 and 40,000 respectively and Russia had 200,000) this number was reduced to about 8,500 in 1950 when the Yugoslav claim on Carinthia had been settled to Austria's advantage (US, France and Russia had 10,000, 6,000 and 44,000 respectively).

As from 1st January 1954, however, the British troops were reduced to a token force of only one battalion. This amounted to one-quarter of the strength of US forces, one-half to that of France, and one-eighth of that of the Soviet Union. Also, as from that date the British and French waived all payment claims to Austria for the military occupation. At 1953 prices the British occupation force cost the Austrian Government some two million dollars per annum. The Soviet Union waived occupation costs on 1st August 1953 and the United States six years previously, in June 1947.

The BTA military route to the British Zone was by land and sea and became known as Medloc "C". The sea crossing was made between Harwich and the Hook of Holland and the rail journey terminated at Villach (Seebach Station) close by Alamein Transit Camp where those troops and personnel proceeding to Vienna or Trieste could stay overnight before continuing their journey. An army bus service ran between Alamein and Trieste, and those travelling to Vienna took the military train which ran nightly. Documents were required on this service, namely Movement Orders (AFW 5178 [BTA]) and Grey Passes, the latter being necessary for entering the Russian zone of Austria. Alternatively it was possible to travel by air between Northolt and Vienna in civil aircraft of BEAC (British European Airways Corporation). Air travel was strictly limited to circumstances such as urgent medical and compassionate cases where the time factor precluded other means of travel. The daily service operating in 1948 for example was by BEAC via Frankfurt and took about seven hours.

Light meals were obtainable on board.

On the Medloc "C" route there were special military trains in the United Kingdom starting at London and York for the convenience of military and official travellers bound for Harwich. On arrival at Parkeston Quay, a meal was provided and documents checked before an evening embarkation for the night crossing by military ship to the Hook of Holland. The crossing took about nine hours. On arrival at the "Hook" a modern transit camp was available to provide meals, washing facilities, welfare shops and cinemas, and for changing sterling into BAFSVs (British Armed Forces Special Vouchers), the money used by military personnel in army shops and NAAFIs (Navy, Army and Air Force Institutes) in Austria. Travellers to Austria had only two hours to spend in the Hook transit camp before starting the thirty-one hour train journey through Holland and Germany to Villach. They were given breakfast at the Hook. From 1948, kitchen cars were included on all trains and hot meals served at regular intervals to all passengers. For those troops who had never been to Austria before the journey was a memorable one with lovely views of the rolling German countryside as the train passed through Bavaria. Berchtesgaden, where it all began in 1938, was clearly visible to the south as the train neared Salzburg. Beyond Salzburg the train passed through some of the most magnificent alpine scenery.

To the young conscript perhaps just out of school or college this last lap of the journey was breathtaking and one he would never forget.

The coaches used on the Medloc "C" route were a very varied collection. Some were Austrian and German, a few Italian and some British. The British coaches were sent to Austria in the summer of 1947 having previously been used on the Medloc "A" route between Calais and Toulon. Originally the continental coaches had hard seats and were in an appalling condition through lack of maintenance. Complete overhaul and refitting was carried out over many months. Couchettes were available for certain ranks. Baggage entitlement was laid down from time to time by the MFO (Military Forwarding Organization) but the normal scale was 112 lbs for officers and 56 lbs for other ranks. Unaccompanied baggage sent through MFO varied in transit time but generally took about three to four weeks. Accompanied baggage was normally taken into compartments with the owner but a baggage van was available on every train, guarded by a military guard throughout the journey.

The organisation of British Troops in Austria and of the Allied

Commission for Austria (British Element) was reviewed in 1948 as a result of the breakdown of the Foreign Ministers' Conference.

The Commander-in-Chief, British Troops in Austria, acted in a dual capacity as such and as High Commissioner. He was therefore responsible to the War Office for British Troops in Austria and to the Foreign office for the working of the Commission and for Civil Liaison in the Zone and in part of Vienna. During the ten years of occupation the successive Commanders in Chief of British Troops in Austria had already become well known figures during the Second World War. General Richard McCreery had commanded the Eighth Army; he was the first Commander in Chief, from 1945 to 1946. General Roy Urquart had commanded the 1st Airborne Division at Arnhem; he was the last Commander in Chief, from 1952 to 1955. The Main Headquarters BTA were located in Schönbrunn Barracks, Vienna (previously in Schönbrunn Palace). The Rear Headquarters BTA were located at Klagenfurt (Tarviserstrasse).

The command and administration of units in the British Zone was vested in the Zone Commander (Brigadier) and the Zone Headquarters were located in the same building as Rear Headquarters.

In order to decentralise local administration in places where units were concentrated, Garrison Commanders or Os.C Troops, each with a small Headquarters were located as follows:

Klagenfurt: Garrison Commander (Lt-Col) Jaeger Barracks

Villach: O.C. Troops (Lt-Col) 316 (Alamein) Transit Camp

Graz: O.C. Troops (Lt-Col Commanding Infantry Battalion) Hawkesworth Barracks

The command and administration of units in Vienna was vested in the Commander Vienna Area (Brigadier) whose H.Q. was in Schönbrunn Barracks.

Permanent stations of Infantry Battalions in the Zone were:

Carinthia: Spittal
Pörtschach
Völkermarkt – Wolfsberg – St Paul

Styria: Graz

Battalions carried out a tour of duty in rotation in Vienna lasting about 8 to 10 weeks.

On the cessation of hostilities in May 1945 the British Military Government moved up into Carinthia with the advancing 8th Army as an integral part of the army organisation. On the withdrawal of the Russians from Central and Eastern Styria at the end of July 1945, the whole of the British Zone of Austria was occupied. Shortly afterwards the British staff of Vienna Command moved into the capital, which became quadripartitely occupied by Russians, Americans, French and British as indicated in the previous chapter.

The organisation of Military Government was uniform throughout the Zone. A Chief Military Government Officer (MGO) was appointed for each of the Provinces, Styria and Carinthia, assisted by a staff of expert administrative and technical officers at Graz and Klagenfurt with two or more MGOs in each Bezirk (County) and each large town.

A British Army MP and a German Army Sergeant controlling traffic in the main square of Spittal, Carinthia, on 24th May 1945.

It was the duty of all these officers to know and work with their opposite numbers in the Austrian civil organisation, to control and guide the Austrian departments, and to implement the policy of the Allied Commission for Austria throughout the Zone. It will be recalled that the tasks carried out were onerous in the extreme. The needs of the occupying army in their relation to the civilian population and authorities were the first of these. Food supply, transport, trade and commerce, agriculture, finance, legal procedure and courts, and thousands of Displaced Persons, were some of the civil problems, not to speak of denazification and re-education of the youth on democratic lines, and assisting the revival of free political parties.

By July 1946 the Austrian Government was in a position to assume greater responsibilities and a large measure of autonomy was formally handed back to them under a Control Agreement.

The name of the British administration in the Zone was changed from Military Government to Civil Affairs and later to Civil Liaison. This was intended to, and did, mark the change of policy. From this time on the work on all levels became more and more advisory and informatory and less and less executive. Nevertheless Civil Liaison in the Zone remained in close touch with the daily life of the people and endeavoured to maintain a state of smooth running relationship between the occupying forces and the Austrian population.

The Civil Liaison Officers, especially those in the towns and Bezirke, were well known and popular figures in their areas. The advice of Civil Liaison was sought on all subjects by British military units, by the Civilian Authorities and by the population as individuals.

The attitude of all branches of Civil Liaison was recognised as being free from partiality or favour.

The Deputy Commissioner was also the Executive Chief of the Allied Commission in Austria and under him there was a Secretariat and Divisions which corresponded to the equivalent Ministries of the Austrian Federal Government. In addition to these there were Special Divisions which dealt with Displaced Persons and Reparations, Deliveries and Restitutions (RD and R). The officers of these Divisions were for the most part civilians and were experts in their field. In 1950, however, a civilian High Commissioner was appointed for the first time and in 1951 the British Legation was raised to the status of an Embassy. Similarly the other Allied Legations also became Embassies.

The British Army of Occupation was dispersed in three areas – the provinces of Styria and Carinthia and the British Zone of Vienna. In Styria and Carinthia the Army was centred around the main provincial towns, in Styria the main concentration being in Graz and in Carinthia, Klagenfurt and Villach.

All three towns sustained damage from Allied air attacks during the war. Klagenfurt suffered 51 bombing raids starting in January 1944 when 1,845 tonnes of bombs were dropped causing damage to 50 per cent of the buildings and killing 526 civilians. In Villach the bombing started a few months later killing 272 people in 40 raids. Some 1,200 tonnes of bombs were dropped causing damage to 90 per cent of the buildings and leaving 4,500 homeless. With the exception of Wiener Neustadt, this was the worst bombing experienced in Austria. The greatest architectural loss was undoubtedly the beautiful Renaissance Town Hall in Villach which was damaged beyond repair.

Before the British arrived in Carinthia, therefore, there was a serious shortage of both food and accommodation and troops found themselves occupying a varied range of "billets". The British ration in Austria consisted of 3,400 calories which compared favourably with the home ration. Up until about 1950 the food situation in Austria was precarious and for this reason the purchase of foodstuffs from Austrian resources by the Army was forbidden. Bread was, however, normally baked by a local baker but the flour was provided by the Army.

Most of the fresh food items were imported from Italy, and a good variety was available from this source. Issues in a given week, according to season, included apples, pears, oranges, mandarins, lemons, cabbage, cauliflower, carrots, onions and turnip.

NAAFI maintained Bulk Issue Stores at Vienna, Graz and Klagenfurt where units and messes could obtain, among other things, additional groceries to supplement the Army ration. Prices were about 15 per cent higher than at home, however, due to the additional cost of packing, freight and insurance but there was a wide range of articles. In conjunction with the local breweries, NAAFI arranged the supply of a palatable beer of the same strength as in the U.K. at 8d (3p) per pint. Wines and liqueurs, mostly French, were allocated monthly usually five or six bottles per entitled person. Whisky and gin were available at 9/3d (46p) and 6/9d (34p) per bottle respectively, although up to 1950 both were rationed to half and one and a half bottles per month respectively. Prices of wines and spirits ranged from 7/- (35p) for Red Wines to Cognacs at 22/9 (113p) per bottle.

The standard rate of exchange of 40 Austrian Schillings to the £1 made prices in the Austrian shops seem exhorbitant but later this rate went up to 60 Austrian Schillings to the £1 and in 1950 to 72 to the £1 due to the devaluation of the Schilling.

NAAFI controlled items included the following:

Cigarettes (9d [4p] per packet of 20)	– 105 per head (male personnel) 85 per head (female personnel) per week.
Chocolate (4d [1½p] per 2 oz bar) Confectionery (2/- – 3/- per lb) [10p–15p]	– (6 oz per head per week
Toilet soap (6d [2½p] per tablet)	– half tablet per head per week

It was an offence to pay locally for services in goods instead of Austrian Schillings and it was also an offence to obtain Austrian Schillings in exchanging BAFSV on the "black market", or by selling goods bought from the NAAFI.

Sport was well organised in the British Zone and several BTA representative teams existed. Soccer matches were played against BAOR (British Army of the Rhine) and the French from their Zone. Rugby matches were held in Czechoslovakia, Italy, BAOR and Innsbruck. One of the social highlights of sport in BTA was the Cricket Week held on the BTA Cricket Field in Klagenfurt. The ground was excellently situated and in good condition, was most picturesque with its surround of trees decked in bunting, marquees dotted here and there and NAAFI keeping thirsty and hungry players and spectators satisfied. Other popular sports included hockey, swimming, lawn tennis, boxing and cross country running. In winter of course skiing and skating predominated.

A weekend Vienna Historical Course was available for all ranks and was extremely popular. The course started at 9 am on the Friday and finished at lunch-time on the Sunday.

There were also leave centres on the Wörthersee for Officers and their families, and on the Ossiachersee for Other Ranks and their families where excellent bathing facilities were available.

Officers and certain categories of Other Ranks (e.g. WOs and Sergeants) were permitted to wear plain clothes on most occasions when off duty in the British Zone but not in Vienna. Travellers on military trains both inside and outside Austria were required to wear uniform whether on duty or not. Owing to the hot summer in Southern Austria, Tropical Clothing or Khaki Drill (KD), was worn from May until mid-September. There were three Officers shops in BTA at the following locations:

Klagenfurt:	No. 2 Obstplatz
Graz:	No. 3 Herrengasse
Vienna:	Schönbrunn Barracks

All entitled personnel were issued with a ration card and a points card. The value of the points card was 100 points a year and, for example, one pair of shoes required 9 points, a shirt 7 points and a Mackintosh 16 points. Examples of the rationing system were:

Every 2 months:	2 handkerchiefs; socks, one pair
Every 3 months:	Pillow slips, one; towels, bath, one
Every 4 months:	Collars, one; drawers, one pair; shirts, one; vests, one
Every 6 months:	Boots, ankle, brown or boots battle dress, pair; sheets, cotton, single, pair; shoes, one pair; ties, one
Every 12 months:	Blankets, GS, one; gloves, one pair; jacket, reefer, waterproof, one; pyjamas, one pair
Every 18 months:	Coats, trench, waterproof, one; Mackintosh, one
Every 24 months:	Greatcoat, one; linings, camel fleece, one

The Army Postal Services functioned in Vienna, Klagenfurt, Villach and Graz and postage stamps, postal orders and National Savings Certificates could be purchased at these Army Post Offices and letters and parcels could be posted. The mail services included an air mail service 6 times a week with a transit time of 4 days average. A surface service operated daily except Saturdays since there was no boat service Hook-Harwich on Sundays. The average transit time for this service was 8 days.

Certain duty-free gift parcels could be admitted into the UK without customs duty or purchase tax. These included food parcels which did not weigh more than 22 pounds and other gift parcels which did not exceed 10/- (50p) in total value, provided they did not contain tobacco, scent or liquer.

Married families quarters consisted of furnished houses and flats in the various towns and surrounding country where troops were stationed. Guidance offered to married families posted to Austria gave the following information:

Except in the better class properties, the Austrian does not provide himself with separate dining and sitting rooms, but is content to use one room for both purposes. The rooms are large and airy and usually efficiently heated either centrally or with the Austrian tiled stove. Open fires and their traditional English mantlepiece are never seen. Half the pleasure of being posted to a foreign country lies in the fact that nearly everything is different, even the everyday items which we take for granted at home. If you have not been abroad before, you will notice as soon as you go into an Austrian house that many things we are used to are missing or are found in some other form; – the electric light bulb screws into its socket, the switch is not moved up and down but is turned round, a tremendous tiled stove has taken the place of the open fire and hearth, while the bed has an oversized pillow as a quilt [Duvet]. If you are used to the country, you will observe that the fields have no hedges round them and that hay, when it has been cut, is hung on poles to dry.

Perhaps the few larger cities may not seem very different at first, but most of the population, apart from the Viennese, live in the country in little villages strung out along the flat narrow valleys or in isolated farms which cling to the steep sides of the high mountains. Until the coming of the motor-bus, travel was a long and weary business and for this reason life there has changed far less as the years have gone by than it has in our own land. In winter, too, deep snow often adds to the difficulties of movement and so the village is still used to providing its own entertainments in the way it has always done. Local choirs and amateur performers are always ready to furnish an evening's programme and travelling theatre groups play their simple comedies in village halls which can scarcely accommodate the audiences which crowd to see them. Music is not treated merely as something which comes out of a gramophone or a loud speaker when a button is pressed; ambition to learn to play oneself is there and in many a cottage the favourite is still the zither, whose tone reminds you of the steel guitar. The land is particularly rich in folk-music of every type from jolly country marches, and sly love songs to beautiful melodies on more serious themes; some of them are known throughout Austria while others are associated with some particular district. Almost everyone sings; if one person unthinkingly starts a tune, it is not unusual for three or four to join in with the appropriate harmonies and they all seem to have a repertoire of hundreds of songs.

Thanks to films and musical comedies, the Austrian "Schuh Plattler" are well-known in many lands, but these mock slapping matches to music are very entertaining to watch. In spite of the influence of the wireless, which has brought modern music and even "swing" to all sorts of unexpected places, the village dance remains a lively and vigorous affair of a type unknown to us. A normal band is made up of two clarinets, a trumpet, a horn and a couple of tubas, while the dances themselves consist almost entirely of quick polkas and waltzes. In spite of the energy these demand, it is not unusual for the dancing to start at two or three in the afternoon and continue without a break until seven or eight next morning.

Such dances are often associated with particular festivals at certain seasons of the year. As at home, New Year's Eve is one of these but there are many more, for the old customs have lingered on in the valleys. Thus Fasching (the period before Lent) is a time of great revelry and masked balls are held throughout the land. Each village has its "Kirchtag", the anniversary of the dedication of the church, while in summer an "Almkirchtag" is not uncommon. This seems to be an excuse for especial merrymaking for, in the words of the well-known Austrian song "On the mountains there is no such thing as sin"; once you have climbed up far enough to leave the last of the forest and reach the mountain pastures, there are no rules and regulations to interfere with your enjoyment.

In the same way many old customs have lived on throughout the centuries and some of them are as popular as ever, even though their origins have long been forgotten. Thus in early December, St Nicolas, with white beard and bishop's robes, may be seen going from house to house accompanied by the Krampus, a terrifying figure with a black face, horns and a long red tongue. The saint will reward the good children while his companion has a rod for those who have misbehaved. At Christmas every house has its decorated tree and on Christmas Eve, the candles are lit and the presents piled around its base are distributed. Early in the New Year the Three Holy Kings may be seen singing their traditional songs in remembrance of the visit of the Three Wise Men to the Infant Christ. And so the year goes on with Easter, Whitsun and the rest each bringing its own customs.

The villages themselves, lying in the shadow of the great mountains, never fail to attract the artist and photographer and it is well-worth while looking closely at some of the old wooden houses, sometimes dwarfed by the huge barns which stand beside them, the farms hung along the steep sides of the valley and the white churches shining against the dark background of the woods. Many an ancient castle, too, stands on its crag as a reminder of the troubled days when the barons fought one another across the land or the danger of a Turkish invasion was a very real threat.

But perhaps its scenic beauty is the chief attraction of the British Zone. Carinthia (Kärnten) in particular is a favourite holiday playground and each year its lakes and mountains draw thousands of people from the cities. The great wall of the Karawanken runs along the Southern border and as you travel westward the mountains grow higher and wilder until, climbing by road almost to the snow line, you can look across the sweep of the Pasterze glacier to the dazzling snows of the greatest of them all, the 12,500ft Gross Glockner. Styria too offers a wonderful variety of rolling countryside and is justly called the "Green Steiermark".

Servants for married families were available through the Civil Labour Unit or in the case of certain large units through the Camp Commandant. Their wages were at the then current Austrian rates which, in 1948/49, for a cook was £4 per month. Servants were entitled to two weeks paid holiday for each year of employment.

Hospital facilities for families were provided at 31 (British) General Hospital Klagenfurt, 70 (British) General Hospital, Vienna and 'A' Field Hospital, Graz. When admitted to hospital wives of Officers were charged at 12/- (60p) per day, children 5 – 14 years at 6/- (30p) per day and children under 5 years at 3/- (15p) per day. Wives of Regular Other Ranks paid 1/- (5p) per day when admitted to hospital for confinement but in all other cases were entitled to free medical and hospital treatment. This also applied to their children if under 14 years of age. Families of Other Ranks serving on non-regular engagements were allowed "as a privilege", medical attention, hospital and dental treatment on the same terms as families of regular Other Ranks. A health insurance scheme was in operation within BTA for payment of hospital charges and was open to all who were required to pay for hospital treatment.

Army schools were established throughout the Zone for children's education and for families of military personnel. The education of children of ages five to fifteen was free. For the benefit of parents who may have left children at boarding schools in the UK, special trains were run to bring the children to Austria for the school holidays. The return fare (1948 prices) varied from £12 to £20 according to the age of the child and included the service of a team of Guides who collected the children in London and handed them over to their parents in Austria.

Families in Austria, whether military or civilian who occupied married quarters were permitted to act as hosts to near relatives for visits up to two months in the case of visitors from the UK, and for longer periods in the case of visitors from overseas. A limited number of such visitors could stay in transit hotels in Vienna with the permission of HQ Vienna Area. Visitors were required to make their own travel arrangements to Austria by one of the civil routes but occasionally Medloc "C" passages were available. Visitors were not allowed to draw BAFSV or to cash cheques in Austria but extra rations were made available on repayment and certain NAAFI facilities were also made available.

The tourist trade in Austria could be said to have started as early as 1948 when military restrictions were lifted. British tourists however were restricted to a £35 allowance from which hotel bills had to be paid. When it is realised, however, that the hotel charge was only one Guinea (105p) a day full board (paid prior to leaving the UK) the £35 allowance was adequate. The food in hotels was good and the shops were reasonably stocked with consumer goods but tea and coffee could only be bought on the black market. The tourist was required to pay 12/6 (62p) per gallon for petrol whereas the price to Austrians was about 3/- (15p). There were 60 hotels set aside for tourists in 29 locations from Innsbruck to Velden. There were none available of course in the Russian Zone.

Austrian civilian support staff were required to service BTA during the occupation period and some of these worked for the British for the whole ten year period:

> *I started to work in Alamein in 1945 just after the Camp was opened and stayed until the troops left Villach. Latterly the Camp was closed and the remaining personnel moved to the barracks in town. After the miserable war years I enjoyed working for the British when for the first time in my life I felt a sense of freedom. I often think back to those years. I shall never forget them.*

* * *

> *I was in a compulsory BDM land army camp in the mountains high above Lienz where news took a few days to filter through. One day, however, in the first week of May 1945, I overheard a local farmer tell our Supervisor that Hitler was dead. I didn't need to hear anymore, this is what I had been waiting for – some excuse to get out. That night along with another girl I secretly packed my suitcase and before dawn we decided to steal out of the camp. We had one more thing to do, however. In the limited leisure time we had during the months we spent up there in the mountains, a few of us had sewn together a red-white-red Austrian flag for the day when we could replace the camp Nazi flag. We enjoyed this little bit of intrigue*

but it was dangerous and the flag had to be carefully hidden. Now the time had come and in the dusk of the morning my friend and I quietly pulled down the red Nazi flag with its swastika centre and hoisted the red-white-red of Austria. We then set off on the road to Lienz. Our suitcases were heavy and Lienz was some miles away but shortly we were caught up by a farmer with his horse and cart who kindly gave us a lift the remainder of the way. The farmer turned out to be a French prisoner of war on his way to the station to pick up supplies. I took French in school and I listened to him in his high spirits telling us that "La guerre est finis" and he would soon be back home in his native Paris. He sang his French songs all the way down the valley and I suddenly realised he was the only person I had met from outside our "Greater German Reich" for seven years. I was eighteen and I wondered about the wasted war years, years that I was determined to forget. As the happy Frenchman sang his Country's songs I wondered if I would ever see his native City. But the sun was rising and the morning was beautiful and I was on my way home at last.

We reached Lienz in mid morning and the roads were literally blocked with German army units retreating from Italy. We were fortunate to get a lift in one of the trucks as far as Möllbrucke. They were heading north to Germany I wanted to go south to Villach. Fortunately I had an Aunt in Möllbrucke and I stayed there a few days to recuperate from my ordeal in the mountains. One morning I was wakened by the engine of a motorbike outside. This was nothing unusual but I chanced to look out of the window and there to my astonishment sitting astride his machine talking to a policeman was a British soldier. It was the 8th of May. That morning I quickly packed my suitcase again and was determined to hitch a lift – this time from the British. I knew that some of these trucks would be heading for Klagenfurt and I was right. It took me some time but because of the heavy suitcase I guess they took pity on me. The conversation with the driver to Villach was carried on in Italian because I knew only a few words in English. Ironically it was Hitler who made

English the first foreign language in Austrian schools. Before that it had been French. And so it happened that later my first job with the British was as an interpreter from Italian to German and German to Italian. I worked for them for three years. I had once seen Hitler in Villach, now I saw Alexander, Montgomery, McCreery, Keightley, Galloway, Winterton, and even Kesselring and Schuschnigg who came to Villach to give evidence in the Guido Schmidt trial for fear of demonstrations in Vienna where the trial was being held.

* * *

My parents decided to leave Rumania before the advancing Russians and we arrived in Carinthia in the summer of 1945. I went to college in Klagenfurt but worked for the British at weekends and during the holidays. I knew very little English but picked it up gradually and very soon began taking it seriously, so seriously in fact that I became a teacher of English in the Gymnasium and finally Director of the school.

* * *

I worked in the Alamein Army Education Office although I was a qualified lawyer but this was the only job I could get after the war. However I have no regrets because I found a happy atmosphere in the office and the work was interesting. I believe the experience stood me in good stead in later years and I ultimately became a Commissioner of Police.

* * *

In the early years of occupation, besides military missions the troops performed many civilian tasks. Bridges and roads had to be built or repaired by the Royal Engineers. This work was carried out quietly unlike the approach of the Russians who insisted that each achievement was accompanied by a grand opening ceremony in the presence of political leaders. The Russians also ensured that full newspaper coverage was given to all Soviet civil engineering works carried out in Austria. Perhaps the most important civil engineering work performed by the Sappers in the British Zone was the reconstruction of the Arnoldstein railway bridge immediately after the war.

On the first anniversary of the British entry into Austria, a Civil National Holiday and commemoration parades were held in most British occupied towns. In Villach, troops of the 17th Field Regiment and of the Irish Brigade, passed down the Hauptplatz (formerly the "Adolf Hitler Platz" during the war) to the music of the Pipes and Drums Band of the Irish Brigade. Lieut Colonel G. A. French Commander the 1st Battalion Royal Fusiliers, took the salute at the march past and was afterwards presented with bouquets by children in Austrian National costume. He was joined by the Burgomeister, Herr Victor Petschink. Members of the Civil Police, Fire Brigade, local hunters and others marched past to the music of the Villach Railway Band (8th May 1946).

BTA relations with the Austrian people were good and every opportunity was taken to cement friendship and understanding in spite of the sometimes onerous duties which the army had to perform. Of all the four occupying Powers it is probably fair to say that the British had much more experience of the kind of public relations necessary to gain the respect of the people. An early example of this occurred at a ceremony in October 1946 when Sir James Steele, the British High Commissioner, handed over a cheque for ten thousand pounds to Chancellor Figl, being the proceeds of a British Army Tatoo held in the gardens of Schönbrunn during the summer. The money was given to provide 2,400 needy Austrian school children a six weeks holiday in the country. The bands of the Royal Irish Fusiliers and the Hampshire Regiment played at the ceremony and one Viennese newspaper wrote next day that the event would always be remembered by the children of Vienna.

Unfortunately Yugoslav border shootings went on well into 1948 and it seemed that Yugoslav frontier guards fired first and asked questions later. In 1947 there was a period in July when 12 frontier murders were committed in a period of 3 weeks. In August 1948 Yugoslav frontier guards shot and killed a woman of 34 who unwittingly crossed the border by a few yards to pick bilberries (blaeberries) in the woods. The kidnapping of British troops who strayed across the unmarked border went on into 1949. A troop train was derailed in Carinthia in August 1947 by bombs placed on the rails, and on the same day another bomb exploded outside the Commandant's office at 138 Brigade HQ Velden.

These were just a few of the dangers which troops of BTA faced in the first few years of the occupation. From 1950 on, however, conditions improved gradually and these dangers disappeared.

On 5th April 1948 the Bishop of Fulham dedicated a stained glass window as a memorial to the presence of the British Troops in Austria and the part played by the 8th Army in the liberation of the Country. The window was installed in the Christ Church in Vienna, the only established British Church in Austria. The rededicated church damaged during the war had been restored. The window was a voluntary gift from those serving in Austria. It was designed and made in England and transported to Vienna. General Galloway, High Commissioner and other representatives from France and the United States were present to see the dedication. The window consists of three large panels and includes figures of St George, St Martin and St

Stephen the patron saint of Vienna, and emblems of the 8th Army, V Corps, the Sixth Armoured Division, the 46th Division and the 78th Division, the first formations to enter Austria. This British memorial contrasted vividly with the monument built by the Russians to commemorate their liberation of Vienna. This is a massive war memorial in the Schwarzenbergplatz (Stalin Platz during the occupation). The concrete structure is 120 feet high and was built by Soviet civil engineers and architects in three months during the summer of 1945. The monument is topped by a bronze figure of a Russian soldier with the Red Flag held high in his right hand, automatic weapon across his chest, and a shield held low in his left hand. The monument became known in Vienna as the "Unbekannte Plunderer" (the unknown plunderer).

The USSR Liberation Statue.
The massive statue commemorating the liberation of Vienna by the Russian Army and in memory of those Russians troops who fell in the siege was unveiled at a ceremony attended by the representatives of the Four Powers. This concrete structure stands 120 feet high in the Schwarzenbergplatz (Stalin Platz during the occupation), and was built by Soviet civil engineers and architects in three months during the summer of 1945. The monument is topped by a bronze figure of a Russian soldier with a red flag held high in his right hand, automatic weapon across his chest, and a shield held low in his left hand.

8

DENAZIFICATION

In the years following the Anschluss, economic advantages in Austria were undeniable. The gearing of Austria into the German war economy virtually eliminated unemployment which had been rampant in the mid thirties. Greater Germany provided Austrian agriculture with both a wide market and a cheap and abundant source of artificial fertilisers. Forestry also benefited from the new market. Credit facilities and new social services made a strong impression with the working classes. However, these advantages were short-lived and the maze of controls and regulations became more stringent as the war progressed. The steady decrease in the purchasing power of the mark showed signs that an economic collapse could not indefinitely be delayed.

Politically the first wave of disillusion came early when the new régime flooded the country with officials from Germany who even shut out the local Nazis from the best appointments and were bitterly resented by the patriotism of the people.

The direct impact of the war on the population had two main effects. It denuded the country of all its young men, with the exception of party officials. As a result, both agriculture and industry became dependent on conscripted foreign labour and, at the same time, the bulk of the most solidly Nazi age groups were removed to the front.

Secondly, the extreme youth, so far from being presented with new opportunities, which had been the chief Nazi bait to the young Austrian from 1933 to 1939, could only look forward to early conscription and probably the horrors of the Eastern Front.

The first months of 1945 made it clear that the German armies were facing total defeat and that eleventh hour rescue with the aid of V-weapons was a vain hope. This produced a catastrophic loss of morale inside the Nazi Party itself and gave birth to the so-called "surrender group" which in Carinthia had the support even of Gauleiter Rainer.

The dominent and unifying factor in Carinthia in the early months after the war, however, was the fear of the Russians and of Tito. This transcended all political divergent tendencies making the presence of

British forces necessary and popular.

An early Nazi revival after the war was unlikely, but there were factors which could have emerged if Allied control was relaxed or if the occupation ended prematurely. The reaction to the Russian occupation in Styria, and certainly in Vienna, might have given way to the belief that the Nazi attitude to "Bolshevism" was justified. The British Military Government was aware of the possibility of some diehard Nazis retiring to their farms to await the day when a new depression would provide the necessary economic basis for radical political developments. It was apparent that generally the over 40s tended to return to their pre-Nazi loyalties. The class of 25 – 35 were almost solidly Nazi but largely absent, prisoners or dead. The very young who gained nothing but misery from the Nazi régime were disillusioned and showed early signs of developing an Austrian national consciousness.

There were, however, some places in Carinthia which the British found to be still very pro-Nazi. Spittal was one such town which was believed to be about 75% Nazi. Eisenkappel was another which was solidly Nazi.

Ernst Fischer, Communist Education Minister in the Renner Provisional Government, in a statement on Austrian radio on 18th June 1945 demanded:

> *... a radical purge of Nazis from Austrian political and economic life and merciless punishment of war criminals and traitors. It is high time a law was passed providing for the ruthless punishment of the whole clique responsible for the war atrocities, concentration camps, torture etc ... strict justice has not yet been meted out to the people who have committed treason against the nation, to the murderers, hangmen and Gestapo officials, the growing forte of the people is indiscriminately directed against all Nazis. It often happens that the small fry come off worse than the big offenders; that is the crux of the matter. We must overcome the Austrian weakness for half-hearted measures if we want to sort out the former Nazi Party members. They must be liquidated so as to open the road to co-operation for the others. This is the only way to solve the Nazi problem in Austria.*

During the early months after the end of the war the purge of Nazis was carried out by the British with all haste and the total arrested personnel in the British Zone between 10th May and 18th August 1945 amounted to 2,913 made up as follows:

HSSPF (Hitler SS)	13
SD (Sicherheitsdienst)	185
RSHA (Reichssicherheitshauptamt)	3
Gestapo	243
Abwehr	44
Ortsgruppenführer	587
NSDAP (Nazi Party)	564
SS Officers	275
SS other ranks	551
SA (Sturm-Abteilung)	249
Gauleiter	6
Hitler Youth (Hitler Jugend)	52
BDM (Bund Deutscher Mädel)	20
Kriminal Polizei	19
Civil Government	28
Miscellaneous	74
Total	2,913

Thereafter and during the immediate post-war years, the Carinthian Provisional Government continued the process of denazification under pressure from the British.

However, during the summer and autumn of 1945 small Nazi groups still roamed the mountains and forests mainly for self preservation rather than for any anti-British resistance. Two Nazi rallies took place on the Gerlitzen in July attended by about 50 people of both sexes. Similar meetings were reported in Klagenfurt and Maria Worth. There was some evidence too that plans had been made for a Werwolf organisation in the Niedere-Tauern in the early days after the war. Local Nazis declared that these were called off by Dönitz, but that they still intended to function in the Russian zone.

Various attempts by individual Nazis to drive a wedge between the Western Allies and Russia by the formation of a rival to the Renner Government had been noted. There was also some evidence that elements of the "surrender group" would try to reinfiltrate into public affairs in due course.

In Germany, denazification was the responsibility of the Allies, but in Austria since the country had a Provisional Government the responsibility was given to that Government. Two denazification laws to this effect were enacted, in 1945 and 1947, which banned the Nazi Party and its military units and prescribed penalties. These penalties could be severe and covered all those who still belonged to the Nazi Party and those who had committed crimes under the Nazi régime. The laws also covered Nazi property which passed into the hands of the Austrian Republic, depending on the circumstances, by way of the Allied Military Governments.

The maximum sentence of death could be exercised on those who did not renounce their Nazi Party membership and their property confiscated and only in exceptional circumstances would the sentence be commuted to imprisonment for terms of 10 – 20 years.

The laws provided for the registration of Nazis from July 1933 to April 1945. All those who between 1st July 1933 and 30th March 1938 and who on reaching the age of 18 became members of the Nazi Party were proclaimed guilty of high treason. This category was liable to imprisonment for 5 – 10 years depending on the severity of the case.

In addition, an Ordnance of the Military Government decreed:

1. No person shall wear or display any of the following

   a) the Swastika (Hakenkreuz)

   b) emblems or badges of the NSDAP (Nazi Party)

   c) any medals or orders presented after the Anschluss.

2. No person shall sing or play "Deutschland Über Alles" and the "Horst Wessel Lied" or any other song, or tune associated with the Nazi Party.

3. No person shall use or display any stamp or seal showing the Swastika or any emblem connected with the Nazi Party.

4. The use of all Nazi slogans and Nazi salutes forbidden.

At the Nürnberg trials in 1946 twenty-two German principles (excluding Robert Ley who committed suicide on 25th October 1945) were charged on four counts: conspiracy to commit crimes, crimes against peace, war crimes and crimes against humanity. They were charged with the death of twelve million people and the death penalty was demanded for all the accused. Martin Borman was tried *in absentia*. Twelve prisoners were sentenced to death by hanging, but Göring committed suicide by biting on a vial of poison a short time before he was due to be executed. Three prisoners were acquitted, including von Papen, a majority decision with which the Soviet judge vehemently disagreed, but three received life sentences including Rudolf Hess. Dönitz received ten years, von Neurath fifteen years and Speer and von Schirach each twenty years. Those actually hanged on 16th October 1946 were: von Ribbentrop, Keitel, Kaltenbrunner, Rosenburg, Frank, Frick, Streicher, Sauckel, Jodl and Seyss-Inquart.

In the immediate post war years the Austrian Government tried some 23,000 Nazis accused of war crimes. Of these, 13,000 were convicted and forty-three received the death sentence.

On 14th December 1946, Joseph Kramer, the "Beast of Belsen" and ten others were hanged by the British for atrocities committed at Belsen and Auschwitz and, in 1947, forty-eight Nazi officers and guards were hanged by the U.S. Army at Landsberg for the mass murders at Mauthausen. Four Nazi organisations were found to be criminal in character at Nürnberg. They were:

1. The Leadership Corps of the Nazi Party.
2. Die Schutz-staffeln (SS).
3. Die Sicherheitsdienst (SD).
4. Die Geheimestaats Polizei (Gestapo).

The Tribunal declined to make that finding with respect to:

5. Die Sturm-Abteilungen (SA).

In accordance with the anti-Nazi laws many Nazis were evicted from flats, houses and estates which had been allocated to them by the Gestapo and party favouritism. Depending on the circumstances, such property would sometimes be confiscated by the Allied forces and later disposed of or returned to the Austrian Government. An example of such a situation arose in the French Zone in Tirol concerning an estate belonging to the Duke of Coburg, who was being held in the US zone of Germany. The estate was purported to be taken over in the name of His Majesty the King on the grounds that it belonged to the Duchess of Kent. A British Officer visited the place supposedly on behalf of Her Royal Highness and took full details of the property, balance sheets, photographs, etc. back to London and arranged for notices to be erected declaring that the estate belonged to the Duchess of Kent. The British Military Government arranged for an investigation to be carried out, and the Bailiff left in charge of the estate showed the investigating officer some of the notices and requested him to report to the Duchess on outstanding problems. The estate in question consisted of a castle, hunting lodge, farm buildings, factor's house, deer forest and chamois ground and shooting rights.

However, the investigation proved the whole thing to be a hoax and the property was passed to the Provisional Government of Tirol pending its eventual disposal.

Under the denazification laws, students who held any position of prominence in Nazi organisations were excluded from University or, in milder cases, admitted only after careful scrutiny of their records. Teachers were rigorously purged and all professors and lecturers were subjected to strict denazification.

When privileges such as freedom of movement throughout the country, without police permits, were introduced in 1946 these did not apply to past members of Nazi organisations.

In Carinthia the British Military Government carried out an inspection of all schools. Of the 1,870 teachers screened, 627 were sacked for their Nazi Party membership or sympathies. It was revealed in these inspections that Fascist anti-democratic teaching was predominant since 1934. The British ordered the withdrawal of all books but because of the lack of paper it took some considerable time to have new books printed. Although evening classes in English were started in the summer the schools were closed, but most were functioning again by October. Slovene was introduced again as a second language in parts of Southern Carinthia. The teaching of this had been stopped by the Germans after the Anschluss. Books from libraries were plundered by the Nazis and some 700,000 volumes were restored or added to the libraries of Carinthia by the British Military Government.

Nazi teaching in the schools during the war had been so intensive that it took nearly a generation to rectify the situation and put the quality of life on a democratic footing. Unfortunately a whole generation of children were made to grow up avoiding the use or understanding of such names or terms as Nazi, Hitler, Gestapo, concentration camp. The cracks were papered over and a whole era forgotten. Perhaps this was understandable to a degree in view of the relentless purges of the early years after the war. It is a fact however, that in Austria although one can find a selection of books on the Allied occupation years, there is a complete lack of literature on the Nazi war or indeed the Nazi era.

> *Each morning we had to greet the teacher with Heil Hitler and present the Nazi salute. Everyone was forced to belong to some form of Nazi organisation, and for the girls the choice was between the Hitler Youth (Hitler Jugend) or the BDM (Bund der Deutschen Mädel). Each organisation had a Nazi uniform and on the two occasions when Hitler visited Carinthia, once just shortly after the Anschluss and again in April 1941 the station platform was lined with Hitler Jugend and BDM. The train stopped briefly on both occasions and we all greeted "our Führer", an Austrian like ourselves, with the Nazi salute. He seemed to revel in the adulation and demonstration of apparent loyalty. The few minutes halt on each occasion was sufficient to satisfy the devoted thousands.*

Today few would ever admit to having been part of that ecstatic crowd. On every Nazi Party occasion, such as Hitler's birthday celebrations on 20th April, every house would be festooned with Nazi flags and banners. Looking back today it is almost incredible what was happening to people but if anyone failed to comply they would be reported. There were informers everywhere. One couldn't even trust one's next door neighbour. Before the British entered Carinthia, however, the flags, banners and memorabilia suddenly disappeared for ever. It is rare today even to find photographs of these "festive" occasions.

Graz, 1938; the Herrengasse dressed with Nazi flags and banners to commemorate the fourth anniversary of the murder of Chancellor Dollfuss. In the background can be seen the covered statue of the Virgin Mary converted by the Nazis into a obelisk complete with a donation box for Nazi funds.

Hitler addresses the ecstatic crowds from the balcony of the Hotel Sandwirt in Klagenfurt during his visit to Carinthia in 1941.

The Soviet Union had begun a Nazi purge in their zone only three days after the fall of Vienna and decreed that all members of the Nazi Party were required to register "within 24 hours". They made a distinction, however, of those joining before the Anschluss and those joining after. All persons belonging to the Nazi Party prior to the Anschluss were imprisoned in a camp and put to work on re-building. They were obliged to wear large swastikas on their fronts and backs. Those joining the Party after the Anschluss were required to report for work at 6 am each morning. By the end of June the Russians had arrested and imprisoned no less than 2,000 Nazis in Styria. In 1946 there were still large numbers of Germans living in Austria, particularly in Vienna and in the Soviet zone. On 8th July the Soviet authorities, without warning, ordered 4,500 Germans out of their zone of occupation. They were required to report to the police station next day with baggage not exceeding 30 lb and ready to leave immediately for the French Zone of Germany. The order did not affect Germans living in Austria before the Anschluss.

When Leopold Figl became Chancellor in November one of the most urgent problems he tackled was denazification. Figl himself, who had served five years in a Nazi concentration camp, declared in a statement issued in March 1946:

Cost what it may we intend that none shall escape us who have committed war crimes . . . My Government has set up a Ministerial committee to rid the country of Nazis . . . Our rule will be to use the greatest severity towards important men and to show rather more leniency towards the unimportant whether workers or minor officials who were merely seduced by their leaders. Very often leaders of business . . . in order to enjoy the favours of the Nazis enrolled their entire staffs in the Nazi Party or SA without asking individuals about it. We cannot make employees who were thus pressed into a Nazi formation do the same penance for it as we shall impose on a director.

Figl's principles and ideals were praised by the Allied Council and the Nazi purge went into full swing over the next two years. Nevertheless, many guilty Nazis escaped the net, often by cunning means, and innocent people made to suffer:

I joined the Party before the Anschluss and this gave me a low Party number. I became a member on the "encouragement" of my superiors at work. If I had not I would have been an outcast in our office. It was very similar to what is happening in Russia today where you need to join the Party if you are the least ambitious and wish to gain privileges. I did very little for the Party except, as an accountant, audit local Party funds. After a year or so I became disillusioned but there was no way out – I could not drop the Party, that was a one way ticket to Dachau. I used to listen to the BBC every night if possible with the sound turned down so low that I was forced to put my ear against the set. My wife used to be so scared that someone would hear it and report me – there were informers everywhere. So it was with using the Hitler salute to greet someone in the street; instead of the old Austrian custom of the handshake; it was abhorrent and

> *ridiculous. I used to give an apologetic neat flick of the wrist which frightened my wife. "Better a Nazi salute than a term in Dachau" she would say. But at the end of the war my superiors, staunch Nazis all of them, had to have a scapegoat and I was he. They were all admonished by cunning means and I was penalised. I was demoted, lost my seniority and was forced to take a large salary cut which I never recovered, and retired 20 years later with half the pension I was entitled to. In spite of numerous appeals I never did regain my status or my pension rights.*

The above statement from a reliable source supports reports circulating at the time that many minor Nazi Party members suffered unnecessarily while others such as senior officials of the Party escaped any form of retribution. Such cases as the above are surprising since on 18th July 1952 as many as seven Bills were passed by the Austrian Parliament which permitted a large scale amnesty for former Nazi Party members as well as compensation for former victims of Nazism. The first law restored full civic and property rights to some 20,000 former Austrian Nazi Party members up to the rank of area chief. The second and third laws restored property rights to former Nazi officials and lifted the embargo on promotion and pay increases for thousands of officials who had been convicted for being minor Nazis during the German occupation. The remaining laws provided for the payment of compensation to victims who were imprisoned in concentration camps by the Nazis.

By the time the Allies left, however, denazification in Austria was on the wane and arrests dried up almost completely in the sixties.

Simon Wiesenthal, the hunter of Nazi war criminals, says that although there have been well over 100 war trials in West Germany in the last 15 years, there have been only a fraction in Austria. Austria, he maintains, has never budgeted for searching out war criminals and the gathering of evidence is costly and requires witnesses, items inserted in newspapers throughout the world, announcements about trials, and so on, all of which is expensive. He asserts that Austria has never really been interested in bringing Nazi criminals to justice. An example of this lack of enthusiasm he maintains was shown by the Socialists in 1971/72 when they dropped hundreds of cases. Since 1970, he says, there have been only 8 trials and 6 acquittals. Two of these concerned two engineers who were in the SS and who built the gas chambers in Auschwitz and also repaired them. According to Wiesenthal there have been no trials in Austria since 1975 although the majority of commanders of extermination camps were of Austrian nationality and many have escaped punishment.

In 1985 the Austrian Government infuriated world opinion when the Defence Minister personally greeted the Nazi war criminal Walter Reder on his repatriation.

Major Walter Reder, an Austrian aged 69, had been sentenced to life imprisonment for the murder of 1,830 civilians by his battalion in Mazabotto, a village between Florence and Bologna, during the Autumn of 1944. By January 1985 Reder had spent 33 years in captivity and was due for release in July. By mutual agreement Reder, a sick man, was handed over by the Italian Government to the Austrian Government on 24th January to complete his sentence. Unfortunately the Austrian Defence Minister, Frishenschlager, decided to personally welcome Reder home to Austria and met the plane with Reder on board in secret at Graz. He lunched him and escorted him by Austrian military plane to Baden for hospitalisation. The meeting was exposed, and a furious reaction was sparked off both in Austria and abroad. Ironically the timing of Reder's release could not have been worse, for next day in Vienna the Austrian Chancellor Sinowitz was due to open the meeting of the World Jewish Congress, and Reder was alleged to have taken an active part in the campaign to exterminate Polish Jews early in the war. Frishenschalager refused to resign, the Government tottered on the brink of collapse, but eight days later the Minister received a vote of confidence and the Coalition was saved. Among his supporters was believed to have been the Landeshauptmann of Carinthia.

The Government had hardly time to recover from this embarrassment when in 1986 the Kurt Waldheim case exploded on a bewildered world. Waldheim, President of Austria, is a former Secretary General of the United Nations Organization and the allegation against him, first brought by the World Jewish Congress, was that he was a member of a German Army Group that murdered thousands of Yugoslavs and organised the deportation of the entire Jewish population of Salonika in Greece which amounted to about one-third of the City. Waldheim's immediate reaction was to claim that he was a student in Vienna at the time. He later admitted that he was still in the army but as an interpreter and knew nothing of the Partisan war nor of the Jewish deportations.

When interviewed on BBC radio, Waldheim said that "what went on went beyond normal rules of warfare" and that he "wasn't involved in this cruel warfare" and:

> *Casualties were on both sides . . . German soldiers had also their casualties . . . there were thousands and thousands of casualties of Germans . . . so please be a little more objective. I deeply regret the way this war took place . . . But I want to state clearly that, first, I wasn't involved in this cruel warfare and, secondly, that casualties were on both sides.*

Bruno Kreisky recommended Waldheim as potential Secretary General of the UN and came to his defence as a friend and colleague, but when he received documents showing that Waldheim had in fact spent the last three years of the war in Yugoslavia and not in Vienna, as stated in his Curriculum Vitae (CV), he was disturbed and telephoned Waldheim:

> *"Listen, you have misled me because three important years have not been in your CV". This was a personal problem for me: it was a personal tragedy, and his answer was also in my view a terrible answer because he said to me: "But look, what happened, it is three years, nothing important – unwesentlich" (without any importance). And my last words of the conversation were "three years of war-making in one of the most cruel parts of the front line is not important for you, is nothing, is zero?"*

In the Spring of 1987 the United States Government barred Waldheim from entering the Country by refusing him a visa and placing him on the "Watch List". Canada followed suit and overtures by the Austrian Chancellor Vranitsky in Washington in May to have Waldheim removed from the "Watch List" were unsuccessful.

The evidence against Waldheim is believed to have come from war crime files held in the UN archives. These were compiled by the UN War Crimes Commission between 1943 and 1948 and are alleged to contain 40,000 names.

But in February 1988, a historical commission set up by the Austrian Government concluded in its 48 page report that there was no evidence that Waldheim was guilty of war crimes although he must have been aware of the Nazi crimes against Jews and civilians during the years 1942 and 1943 and apparently offered no protest.

The Waldheim affair brought anti-semitism to the surface in Vienna for the first time in 40 years and broke a conspiracy of silence. Hate mail and dozens of letters were apparently received by the magazine "Die Gemeinde" during the Presidential election of which the following are examples:

Hitler was right he should have gassed you all
and
You dirty Jewish pigs you are not even worthy to lick Waldheim's riding boots (Sic)

The Jews contend that Austria, unlike Germany, has never admitted her true role in the Second World War. She didn't have to declare her guilt, they maintain, because in order to separate the two countries it suited the Allies to treat her as Hitler's victim not Hitler's conspirator and source of inspiration. "Young people demand to know more but since the Waldheim affair older people at last find it's acceptable to be proud of the part they played in the war."

During the Waldheim campaign, the Jews say that anti-semitism was revealed in cunning ways. Big yellow posters (equivalent to the yellow star) shout at the reader.

We don't let others determine who is to be our President, we will decide.
or
Elect a real Austrian.

Yet Kreisky was a Jew and he was appointed Chancellor. It is estimated that there were some 200,000 Jews in Austria before the Anschluss and of those the Nazis murdered 65,000, the remainder either fled, were deported, or survived concentration camps. Their 100,000 apartments were taken over by the Gestapo and the Nazis. In 1945 only 10,000 had returned.

At the end of the war there were nearly 600,000 Nazis in Austria. Together with their families they amounted to about one quarter or one third of the total population. They were not permitted to vote in the 1945 Austrian elections but in the 1949 elections they formed an important floating vote whose favours were canvassed by both the Conservatives (Peoples Party) and the Socialists (Social Democrats). Under the Austrian coalition system of Government, a *Proporz* system had been devised which required an equal number of civil and public servants to vote for each Party. The Socialists, however, had difficulty in filling their quota and conveniently took large numbers of Nazis into their ranks to fill important posts.

When Bruno Kreisky was elected Chancellor it was alleged that he appointed ex-Nazis to his cabinet, but Kreisky recalls:

> *There were very few, some had become honest democrats. In a democratic society, a head of a government has [an] obligation to respect the state of justice. In Austria [you] have to give the members of Nazi Party young men [a] chance to overcome their past. It's always [in] the interest of a Party to get as many votes as possible [and] I have personally said in all campaigns we want the votes of all who are for our political ideas. If not we can accept the votes [from those] who are not Socialists but who are willing to go part of the way with us.*

The loss of just two seats in Austrian politics can be a disaster, and the power wielded by this former Nazi group has perhaps been significant.

Simon Wiesenthal at the age of 80 is still ceaselessly working from his office in the centre of Vienna. While older Austrians may have hidden their past, he is a lone figure exposing war criminals and bringing them to justice. He examines the evidence meticulously, follows up leads and never makes accusations until, in his own words, "my case is iron". His most notorious case was Adolf Eichmann; 80% of Eichmann's staff, he says, were Austrian. From time to time, therefore, a new Nazi accusation or war trial suddenly hits the headlines. When Bower published his book *The Paperclip Conspiracy* in 1987 the media in Britain rushed into print. The *Sunday Mirror*, under the headline "Skeleton in our Cupboard" commented:

> *Before our troops were demobbed, before our blitzed homes were re-built, while the world was still reeling from the horrors of the concentration camps, Nazis were finding sanctuary in Britain.*

> *Evidence is building up that Britain gave refuge to war criminals, men who had helped Hitler to commit some of the vilest atrocities in human history.*
> *Britain was not alone, America, Russia and France joined in a race to scoop up scientists as Germany collapsed.*
> *The skills that they dedicated to the Nazi military machine could be put to use by the Allies' post-war defence industries, on either side of the Iron Curtain.*
> *Because they were useful, the British Government of the day hid them away from justice.*
> *They were protected from prosecution. And the public was never told about them.*
> *Every Government since then has kept the secret of the back-door deals which let them find safety in Britain.*
> *These Governments must have had what they considered good reasons.*
> *But the fact that they kept them secret shows that they did not trust them.*
> *Now one corner of the veil of secrecy has been lifted the Government must strip it away completely.*

The Paperclip Conspiracy was so named because it is alleged that United States interrogators selected German scientists by slipping a paperclip on their personal files. Bower alleges that there were some 600 German scientists who had worked for Hitler but were reclassified as respectable by the Americans, the most notable of which was the Nazi V2 rocket expert Werner von Braun. He also claims how the United States space programme was achieved with their help.

An all party Parliamentary War Crimes Group published their report in December 1988 documenting how the thousands of Ukranian Waffen SS, referred to in Chapter 3, entered Britain in 1947 from camps in Italy. According to the report many of these may have participated in mass extermination. A Committee set up by the Home Secretary, Douglas Hurd to establish whether any suspected war criminals were still living in Britain is expected to publish its report in 1989.

The World Jewish Congress estimate at least 10,000 Nazi war criminals managed to enter the United States and Rabbi Hier, dean of the Yeshiva University in Los Angeles, which houses the Simon

Wiesenthal Center for Holocaust Studies, believes it is a mockery that only about 6,000 Nazis have ever been sentenced for war crimes.

Almost at the same time as *The Paperclip Conspiracy* was making news, the Government had to deal with allegations made by the Simon Wiesenthal Center in Los Angeles that there were seventeen alleged Nazi war criminals living in Britain. The names of these were given to the Prime Minister in October 1986, but no action was taken until February 1987 when the Home Secretary confirmed that at least six of the men on the list were living "in our midst", two were probably still alive, three were dead and six were untraced. It was believed that some had come as refugees but others with the connivance of the post-war government, and most of them settled down to lead successful lives in industry and the professions. It is not known how many, if any, of the seventeen were Austrians, but also in February Scottish Television in a documentary stated that the Russian Government had supplied them with a dossier listing a further thirty-four Nazis who fled to Britain after the Second World War. The dossier states that these men were responsible for the mass execution of British servicemen, Jews and partisans held in Nazi occupied Russia. The groups of seventeen and thirty-four were believed to have committed a series of crimes in Lithuania and Latvia, where there were over 300,000 Jews before the war but only a few thousand survivors at the end of it, and in the Ukraine where it is alleged 46,000 Jews were massacred. Also in February the trial of John Demjanjuk in Jerusalem replayed the horrors of the holocaust this time in Treblinka where it is alleged 900,000 Jews were murdered. Demjanjuk was accused of being the camp guard who was so brutal that inmates called him "Ivan the Terrible". But Demjanjuk was neither German nor Austrian – he was a Ukranian Nazi. After a trial lasting over a year, Demjanjuk was found guilty and sentenced to death.

On 3rd July 1987 Klaus Barbie aged 73, the former Lyons Gestapo chief and who had become better known as the "Butcher of Lyons" was sentenced to life imprisonment for war crimes. He was found guilty of among other accusations, deporting 844 people to Nazi extermination camps. Of these 373 were murdered in the gas ovens.

Karl Linnas, a 67 year old Estonian, was convicted *in abstentia* by the Soviet Union in 1962. As a former Nazi camp commandant he was found guilty of being directly involved in the murder of 12,000 prisoners. Linnas had lived comfortably in the United States since 1951, but in April 1987 he was finally deported to the Soviet Union to face sentence which inevitably would have meant a firing squad. On 2nd July he died in a Leningrad Military hospital before sentence could be carried out.

In November 1987 the Austrian Josef Schwammberger, an alleged Nazi war criminal and wanted in West Germany on genocide charges, was arrested by Argentine security forces. Schwammberger was actually arrested in West Germany in 1947 but escaped a year later and is believed to have fled through Austria and Italy and helped in doing so by the Odessa organisation.

After nearly 50 years the Nazis who committed war crimes are still being relentlessly pursued by the World Jewish Congress. Hitler said his Reich would last for a thousand years. It only lasted seven, but it will be remembered perhaps for a thousand.

9

REBIRTH OF A PROUD NATION

It took the Allies ten years to sign the Austrian treaty. The reason for this monstrous delay in granting Austria her freedom and independence was caused by Soviet intransigence and blackmail. The main issue concerned the definition of German assets in Austria which the Russians were claiming as reparations. At the time of the Anschluss, Hitler decreed that all Austrian Government property was German property including the seizure of British and American firms. The Three Power conference in London in 1943 agreed that the Allies would co-operate to return stolen property to its rightful owners. At Potsdam it was further agreed that Russia should be given as reparations all German property in their zone of occupation. The Russians never lived up to this agreement and declared almost everything the Germans had stolen in Austria was legitimate German property and should be returned to the Soviet Union as reparations. This included many thousands of acres of training grounds, mineral rights, property of foreign nationals and property seized from the Jews. Most important were the Zistersdorf oil fields in which the United States and Britain held almost 50 per cent of investment. As far as the Soviet Union was concerned her approach to reparations was to claim everything and then challenge the Austrians and the other Allied Powers to prove that it had not been German property. In this way they removed vast amounts of material from Austria in a period of looting which all but wrecked the Country's economy. Some 300 industrial enterprises were seized of which only half could be considered as German owned. The Russians therefore refused to sign a treaty unless it included a clause that legalised their rape of the Austrian economy.

General Clark, the US High Commissioner for Austria and former Commander of 15th Allied Army Group in Italy under the Supreme Commander Field Marshal Alexander, expressed his feelings in his book *Calculated Risk*.

> *It is clearly evident to me that the Soviet policy is to prevent establishment of Austria as an economic entity without*

> *strong ties to Soviet territory or Soviet-controlled areas. While the Governments of the three Western Powers are attempting to reach agreement on the vital question of German assets, the Soviets are removing many important plants, resources, and other economic assets from their zone. In other cases, such as the Zistersdorf oil-fields and the Danube Shipping Company, they are taking over control in such a way that Austria must remain dependent upon Soviet influence for years to come.*

Clark maintained that the Russians were ready to resort to lying, to betrayal, and to the repudiation of solemn pledges and thought that they were accustomed to the use of force. They were also skilled in exploiting any sign of weakness or uncertainty or appeasement as part of their national policy. Clark once said to Konev, the Russian High Commissioner for Austria: "You've made ten demands at this Council meeting that we can't meet. But suppose I should say 'All right. We agree to all ten demands.' Then what would you do?" "Tomorrow," he said, "I'd have ten new ones."

On several occasions over the years the problem became so serious that the Western Allies were almost resigned to Austria being partitioned, like Germany still is today, into West and East with Vienna a divided city like Berlin and surrounded by the Russian zone of occupation. It is probably true that the Soviet Union had hopes of making Austria into another Soviet satellite, like Hungary, and it was not for the lack of opportunity that they failed. They were first into Austria and first into Vienna and they had prepared politically for the situation by "entertaining" in Russia throughout the war several Austrian Communist leaders. The three General Elections during the occupation, however, emphasised that the Austrians were having none of it, for out of a total of 165 parliamentary seats, in 1945 the communists obtained only 4 seats; in 1949 they managed one more, but in the 1953 election, although they formed an alliance with the People's Opposition (VÖ) they again obtained only 4 seats. These results must have disheartened the Kremlin and probably had a bearing on their search for an excuse to pull out of Austria without losing face.

The first attempt to draft a treaty took place in Potsdam in 1945. The agenda for the conference had been drawn up having as the first item the Italian Treaty and the second the Austrian Treaty. For two years thereafter the Soviet Union refused to discuss item 2 until item 1 had been concluded. Bevin and Byrnes, US Secretary of State tried again in the following year at the Foreign Ministers' meeting in Paris but Molotov refused. It began to appear to the Western Allies that the Soviets were doing so well from milking the Austrian economy that they did not see any undue hurry to end the occupation. Besides, by keeping their large army in Austria, at the Austrian Government's expense, they would be able to retain their troops in Hungary and Rumania with the excuse that they were protecting their lines of communication to Austria.

Bevin later in the year told the House of Commons:

The Soviet Union argued that they were not ready to discuss Austria. I could not understand this, and I do not understand it now.

The Austrian Treaty negotiations with the Soviet Union were the first serious discussions between East and West after the war and Bevin would not be the last Foreign Minister who would "not understand" Soviet intransigence.

The next opportunity for the Foreign Ministers to discuss the treaty was at the Moscow Conference in the Spring of 1947. At this meeting both the Austrians and Yugoslavs were invited to send delegations. Later the Austrians would remark that out of the 720 hours of the conference, they spent 716 of them in their hotel rooms. The Yugoslavs, however, took the opportunity to present their case for the cession of Carinthian territory and $150 million in reparations. These claims were strongly supported by the Soviet Union. In an endeavour to break the deadlock an Austrian Treaty Commission was appointed which, by April 1948, had met one hundred times without finding a solution.

The Communist coup in Czechoslovakia and the Berlin blockade both affected the progress towards an Austrian treaty in 1948. The former gave the Western Allies second thoughts in being too hasty in concluding a treaty that would leave Austria without protection, and the latter may have given the Soviet Union ideas to introduce a similar blockade in Vienna. Indeed, for a few months during the spring and summer, travel to and from Vienna from the Western zones of occupation was severely restricted by the Russians. Although the restrictions were lifted by the autumn, anxiety continued for some months. There was however a further event in 1948 which was to have a singular effect not only on the Austrian treaty but on Yugoslavia's claim on Carinthia. This was the break between Stalin and Tito in June which resulted in Yugoslavia being expelled from the Cominform. There had been rumours over previous months that a breach in relations had taken place between the two leaders. Tito's determination to prevent Soviet domination and exploitation of his country was believed to be the main reason for the rift, but Stalin considered that Tito had reoriented his Communist government towards the capital democracies. The Yugoslav leader characterised his rule as genuine Marxism-Leninism and charged that the roots of the new society planted in the Soviet Union under Lenin had "completely withered in the soil of a backward, despotic, Asiatic dictatorship".

According to Dedijer, however, Molotov and Vyshinski told Kardelj in Dedijer's presence at the Moscow Conference in 1947 that there was not the slightest chance of Yugoslavia's territorial demands on Carinthia being accepted. It was evident to Dedijer that Stalin was ruthlessly using the Carinthian Slovenes to bargain for some $150 million of German property in Austria.

Because of the break in Soviet-Yugoslav relations it was naturally felt by the Western Allies that Russia would no longer continue to support Yugoslavia's claims on Carinthia and so ease at least one logjam towards agreement. This turned out not to be the case and for the remainder of 1948 the Soviets maintained their support not only for Yugoslavia's claims against Austria but also Yugoslav charges against the British and Americans in Trieste. To get this far had taken fourteen Foreign Ministers' Conferences.

At the Foreign Ministers Deputies' meeting in London on 1st July 1949 the Soviet Union at last withdrew its support for Yugoslavia's territorial claim on Carinthia. This outstanding claim was thereupon formally rejected by the Deputies, and although Yugoslavia would strongly object to the decision and maintain her pressure for a satisfactory compromise, without the Soviet Union's backing there was little chance of success now. The decision was a victory for the Western Allies but especially for Ernest Bevin who, since taking over as Foreign Minister, was adamant that Carinthia would remain in Austria, not just part of it but all of it.

Under the dangerous situation prevailing in the British Zone in the immediate post war period and the limited resources available to the British, it might have been easier, or even convenient, for a lesser Foreign Minister to appease the Yugoslavs. The Moscow Declaration and the Atlantic Charter were all very well in theory but the combined pressure imposed by the Soviet Union and Yugoslavia, could well have been grounds for appeasement. It is doubtful if public opinion in either America or Britain would have been aroused if the Yugoslav claim had been agreed in some form. There had been no outcry over the return of the Cossacks, and it was extremely unlikely that Carinthia would have stirred public opinion at home. The war was over and people just wanted to get on with their lives.

Marshal Tito, however, was moved to state in a speech on 10th July at Pula that Yugoslavia would not renounce her claims on Slovene Carinthia. He refuted Soviet allegations that Yugoslavia had two years earlier negotiated "behind the back" of the Soviet Union with "Foreign Imperialists" over Carinthia. He declared that the Soviet Foreign Minister Vyshinsky pronounced a gross falsehood. It was not true, he said, that Yugoslavia had ever reached agreement on Carinthia with the Imperialists without the knowledge of the Soviet Union . . . It is they (the Soviets) who have sold Slovene Carinthia and therefore it is they who bear all responsibility. "We have not renounced our right to Carinthia, nor shall we ever renounce it."

In May 1950 the Soviet Union replaced Carinthia with the Trieste question and made it clear at a meeting in London that it had no intention of concluding an Austrian treaty until the Trieste problem was resolved in Yugoslavia's favour and claimed that Austria was still harbouring Nazis. This news came as no surprise to the Austrian Government who long ago concluded that Russia had changed her mind about granting a treaty and was seeking every excuse to disguise this fact.

By the end of the year fourteen out of fifty-three articles of the draft treaty had still to be approved and almost all of these concerned the Soviet claim on reparations and German assets. The Foreign Ministers' Deputies had now chalked up 250 meetings. During the next three years, even though Stalin had died and Malenkov had taken over, there was little progress, and the Soviet Union presented additional irrelevent proposals to obstruct further negotiations.

However, on 30th October 1953, the 10th anniversary of the Moscow Declaration was marked throughout Austria by a five minute stoppage of work as a protest against the Four Powers' failure to restore Austrian independence and freedom as promised in the Declaration. Dr Raab, the Federal Chancellor said of the occasion:

> *Austria would not consider itself free until the last soldier had left Austrian soil. It is unfortunate today that our country has become a bargaining counter in the hands of the Great Powers and that not one of them whether for strategic or prestige reasons will abandon the occupation. Though Austria had been very patient, she now told the world in the most powerful demonstration since the end of the war that she was unwilling to bear the present position any longer.*

Dr Raab described the Soviet Union policy as grotesque that Austria was having to buy back oil which had lain under Austrian soil for thousands of years. He maintained that the Russian policy of declaring property seized by the Nazis as German assets meant legalising Hitler's robbery of Austrian property.

A four-Power conference in Berlin in February 1954 once again confirmed the intransigence of the Soviet Union. The three Western Foreign Ministers offered to accept the Soviet version of all outstanding Articles but Molotov suddenly produced new conditions. He now insisted that even after an Austrian treaty had been concluded the occupation troops should remain in Austria until a German peace treaty was agreed. This, according to Molotov, was to guard against any German designs for another Anschluss. He declared that 1½ million Austrians had fought in the German Army during the war and that 17 Austrian divisions fought on the Russian front. France suggested at the United Nations General Assembly in November that in the interests of goodwill the Four Powers should conclude an Austrian Treaty which could provide for the Allied troops to remain in Austria for 18 months to two years after conclusion of the treaty instead of the 90 days proposed in the draft. In a note to the Austrian Goverment in December, however, the Soviet Union again issued a warning of the increasing danger of Anschluss attempts after the rearming of Germany. For some reason Soviet propaganda concentrated throughout the year on the alleged danger of an Anschluss. It may have been a visit to Austria by Field Marshall Kesselring in March which aroused fear in Moscow. Also, towards the end of the year a judgment issued by the Federal German Administration Court that, in German law, Austrians were still German nationals since the Anschluss law of March 1938 had never been removed from the German statute book. It can be imagined what this sort of statement would have had on the suspicious Soviet mind. Nevertheless it was something that could cause a further reason for delay in concluding the treaty and steps were taken by the Federal German Government to declare the Anschluss null and void. In doing so they adopted a law which allowed Austrian residents in Germany to opt for German nationality.

The year 1955 saw the break-through. It came suddenly and at the instigation of the Soviet Union. An Austrian delegation was summoned to Moscow in April and told that Russia would sign a treaty and withdraw its occupation forces if Austria would undertake to declare a state of neutrality.

The point was that a neutral Austria left a 530 miles long wedge separating Italy from West Germany which split NATO and the Western defence in two. The supply and communication lines between Germany and Italy which ran through Tirol would be cut and this prospect undoubtedly upset the Western Allies. They were not enthusiastic about the arrangement and there is no doubt that they had hoped that Austria would have joined the Western Alliance upon the granting of independence. The cost in reparations was of little account to the Western Allies if Austria could be wooed to join NATO. In years to come the Soviet Union would remind Austria that Soviet forces were withdrawn from Austria on the guarantee of this neutrality. In 1988 this was put to the test when Austria decided to apply for full membership of the EEC and President Gorbachev politely reminded the Austrian Chancellor Dr Franz Vranitzky of the guarantee and the Soviet veto which he was determined to use.

The Soviet Government would also make concessions in certain clauses of the treaty. The $150 million could be paid in the form of goods at an annual rate of $25 million, the Danube Shipping Company would be returned to Austria for a payment of $2 million in cash and the oil fields and refineries returned for the payment of 10 million tons of crude oil over ten years. Oil and shipping property would also be returned upon payment of 600 million schillings (about $30 million). On this basis it was estimated that about 20 per cent of Austrian exports and 10 per cent of her imports would be tied to trading with the Soviet Union and her satellites. Nevertheless it was a price which Austria was willing to pay for independence. On their return to Vienna from Moscow the Austrian delegation, led by the Chancellor Raab, drove from the airport to the City amid enthusiastic scenes of cheering crowds.

The twist in fortunes after almost ten years of fruitless discussion was ironic because a neutral Austria was advocated by Austria on many occasions over the years since the war. The first public statement on possible neutrality came from President Renner in 1947 who pointed to Switzerland as being a model for Austria. It was followed by a unanimously adopted resolution at the Socialist Party's annual conference. Renner's successor Theodor Körner also declared for Austrian neutrality in 1951 and Foreign Minister Karl Gruber in 1952. In 1954 neutrality was even approved by the Four Powers at the Berlin Conference of Foreign Ministers – at the suggestion of Molotov. So the case for a neutral Austria was not new by any means.

Harold Macmillan was now British Foreign Minister and he set off for Vienna to sign the Austrian Treaty on 13th May exactly ten years to the day since he first flew to Klagenfurt for his eventful meeting with General Keightley:

> *The weather was perfect, with bright sun but not too hot. The people were in a very gay mood, looking forward with delight to the prospect of the end of the occupation after ten years. The British had only a token force of one battalion, but the Americans had 20,000 troops and the Russians double or treble that number.*
> *On the morning of 14th May I went with the British Ambassador, Sir Geoffrey Wallinger, to call upon the Austrian Chancellor, Dr Julius Raab. The Foreign Minister, Dr Leopold Figl, was present. They were housed in Maria Theresa's old palace – a lovely building. Both were in a state of barely suppressed excitement. Could it really be true that the Russians (with their 40,000 – 60,000 troops in this small country) could perhaps be gone by the autumn? After a general talk, we were shown round the lovely rooms of this palace, including that in which the Peace Treaty of Vienna was actually signed. This is the room with the five doors, specially built so that the Tsar and the Emperor of Austria and three kings could enter the room simultaneously – a splendid solution to the problem of precedence.*
> *. . . A lovely sunny day; the streets full of happy people; cheers and hand-waving as our car passes, with the Union Jack. Great crowds outside the Allied Control building. They cheered, clapped and waved, as I got out. I stood on*

the steps, bowed, waved, etc. as the photographers clicked their cameras and the radio reporters did their stuff.

The formal signing of the treaty took place on the following day in the octagonal hall of marble and gilt in the Belvedere Palace. Mr Molotov and the Soviet delegation were first to arrive at 11 am to greet the members of the Austrian delegation already assembled. They were followed at seven-minute intervals by Mr Macmillan and the British delegation, the United States delegation led by Mr Dulles and Mr Pinay and the French delegation. After an exchange of greetings Dr Figl and the Ministers with their Ambassadors each sat on gold and white chairs – nine in all – at a row of similarly coloured tables covered with cerise-coloured cloth in front of nine leather blotters and nine gold-topped fountain pens in stands.

The treaty consisted of a massive volume of 70 pages bound in green morocco leather with gold tooling and was signed by the Ministers and their Ambassadors in order of precedence according to Austrian protocol. Russia signed first, followed by Britain, the United States, France and, last, Dr Figl signed for Austria. The treaty had been bound by the same Viennese firm of bookbinders which had bound the treaties of the Congress of Vienna in 1815 when Swiss neutrality was first declared. Each of the four Foreign Ministers received as a momento of the occasion a collection of stamps boxed in embossed red leather.

After the signing the Foreign Ministers went out on to the balcony and received an enthusiastic welcome from thousands of people assembled in the Palace gardens. This was a happy joyful crowd so very different from that of seventeen years before which had assembled to greet the Führer.

We all went repeatedly on to the balcony facing the gardens. The immense crowd greeted all the Foreign Ministers (at their various appearances) with wild applause. I thought Molotov got most applause! Perhaps because they will be so glad when the Russians – all 60,000 of them – finally go away . . .

In the speeches that followed Mr Macmillan said:

A very great honour has fallen to me today – the honour of

signing this long awaited treaty in the name of the Queen, my gracious Sovereign. It is a great honour, and a great good fortune for me to have been able to take some small part in the closing weeks of its 10-year history. But it is only right that I should pay tribute to the patient work in connection with the treaty of the eminent men who preceded me at the Foreign Office – the late Mr Ernest Bevin, Mr Morrison and our present Prime Minister Sir Anthony Eden. [In two more years Macmillan himself would become Prime Minister.]
Over the last 10 difficult years the Austrian people have shown their constancy and courage. Under their coalition Government they have achieved great progress. Today's ceremony marks the beginning of a new epoch for Austria. It is a happy day for all of us. But for Austria itself it is also a day of challenge. In meeting that challenge she will know that she can always rely on the warm and steady friendship of the British people.

Mr Macmillan received loud applause from everyone assembled.

After the ceremony the Foreign Ministers drove through the beflagged streets, cheered by crowds, to be entertained at luncheon by Dr Körner, President of Austria at his residence in the Hofburg, the former imperial palace.

Mr Macmillan again:

There followed an immense luncheon with a vast number of people in the royal palace, in the old wing once occupied by Maria Theresa. It began at 2 pm and ended at four.
Pinay and I (not Dulles or Molotov!) then went to the Te Deum, which was beautifully sung before all the civil and ecclesiastical notables, in the Cathedral Church of St Stephen.
After a short interval we all had to start off again, in evening clothes, for a dinner at the Schönbrunn Palace at 7 pm.
This was in a splendid hall, again with lovely gold plates (we had much of this at the luncheon) and lovely china – belonging, I suppose, to the Imperial House. The flowers were wonderful also. (This is a specially good time for

Vienna – the lilacs are all out in the city streets, gardens, and much other blossom as well.) The toasts were short. We each gave one in turn.
There followed a reception, with over 2,000 guests, in the ballroom of the Schönbrunn Palace. Among the guests were the Cardinal, and the Archbishop and other ecclesiastics . . . in full splendour. Molotov was introduced to them, but seemed rather embarrassed.

Macmillan thought that many politicians "flattered ourselves" that the situation marked a change of heart in the post-Stalin period. However, he considered it more likely that the Austrian treaty was used as part of the game of power politics which followed Stalin's death. As a sign of this it was announced a day before the signing of the treaty that a State visit to Yugoslavia would be undertaken by the Soviet leaders. The strong delegation would include Krushchev, Bulganin, Mikoyan and Shepilov but no Molotov. Macmillan suggests that this rebuff and others which were to follow were intended to weaken Molotov and eventually lead to his downfall. Molotov, according to Macmillan, stood for orthodox Communism while Krushchev was seeking a more flexible policy.

On the 25th anniversary of the signing of the treaty in 1980, Macmillan and the only other survivor of the co-signatories present, the former French Foreign Minister M. Pinay, teasingly inquired of Gromyko "Whatever happened to our dear old colleague, Monsieur Molotov?" Pinay received the appropriate retort "Il est libre, mais tres malade!"

On the eve of the signing of the Austrian Treaty the Warsaw Treaty was signed in Moscow establishing a unified command in eastern Europe. Nevertheless there seemed good reason to believe that Krushchev saw withdrawal from Austria as strengthening his argument for German reunification later in the year, especially since West Germany was about to join NATO. If Germany could be reunited and neutral like Austria she would offer great advantages to Russia. Moreover Austria was not a serious military loss to Russia. Indeed it might have the advantage of creating a neutral Swiss – Austria belt separating NATO forces in Italy and West Germany as indicated above.

There was also little encouraging signs from the electorate that there was any indication of a move towards Communism. After ten years of occupation Austrian politics remained substantially stable. In fact during the previous October's Provincial elections in four of the Provinces (Länder) Vienna, Lower Austria (in the Soviet Zone), Salzburg and Vorarlberg, the Communists made no headway and the great bulk of the votes went to the two Coalition parties. The Communists lost one of their seats in Vienna and had to make do by retaining their three seats in Lower Austria. In the other two Länder they were again unrepresented.

In the final version of the treaty, union with Germany was forbidden by Article 4 and Russia dropped Article 17 which had limited Austria to an army of 53,000 men and an air force of 90 aircraft. At the eleventh hour and at Figl's request the Austrian war guilt clause in the preamble was also dropped – a final gesture from Molotov who was soon to fall from grace in the Soviet hierarchy.

The rights of the Slovene and Croat minorities in Carinthia, Styria and Burgenland were preserved under Article 7 of the treaty. They were to enjoy the same rights on equal terms as all other Austrians including the right to their own organisations, meetings and press in their own language.

They would be entitled to elementary instruction in the Slovene or Croat language and to a proportional number of their own secondary schools.

The Slovene or Croat language would be accepted as an official language in addition to German in areas of Carinthia, Styria and Burgenland where there was a mixed Slovene or Croat population. In these districts, the Slovene or Croat language would be used in topographical terminology and inscriptions as well as in German, and Austrian nationals of the Slovene and Croat minorities would be permitted to participate in the cultural administrative and judicial systems on equal terms with other Austrian nationals.

This Article perhaps did not entirely satisfy Yugoslavia whose territorial claims were lost, perhaps for ever, but it went a long way conceding to Yugoslav demands for the minorities in those districts. Now, over 30 years later the matter of minority rights is again causing concern in Slovene Carinthia.

In discussion with the Yugoslav Institute in Klagenfurt in the Spring of 1987, the author was informed that the education rights of the Slovene minorities in Carinthia, as laid down in Article 7 of the Treaty, were no longer being observed by the Austrian Government. Representation on this score was being made by the Institute but later in the same year large scale demonstrations were held by the Slovene minorities denouncing Government policy on the issue. The problem is perhaps best illustrated by the following observation from a native of Southern Carinthia:

> *I went to school in the area of Southern Carinthia where both Slovene and German is spoken by many people [the area is known as "Slovene Carinthia" by Yugoslavia and the "dual language region" by Austria], and until I was nine years old was taught only in the Slovene language. However, after the Anschluss the Slovene language was banned by Hitler and for the rest of my schooling I was taught only in German and gradually forgot my Slovene although my parents still spoke Slovene at home as well as German. Today I am Director of a College not far from where I went to School but only German is spoken in my native village now. My brother is younger than me, and since the Slovene language was re-introduced to schools in the area immediately after the war during the British occupation, he is today fluent in both Slovene and German. His children, however, can only speak German.*

Austria's proposed declaration of neutrality and her intention to join the United Nations, as agreed in Moscow in April, raised several questions. It was recognised at the same time that the Soviet idea of a neutral Austria would be a useful pattern for Germany to copy if or when she obtained reunification. It would also prevent Austria from joining NATO. However if Austrian neutrality was based on the Swiss model it was noted that Swiss neutrality was not even recognised by either the Soviet Union or the United States. Moreover during the war neutrality had always been denounced by Russia.

Switzerland was not a member of the United Nations but could Austria become a member and still be neutral or would it conflict with the UN Articles of Membership? Under the UN Charter her obligations would prevail and a State which merely participated in collective Charter action in restraint of aggression was not considered as departing from neutrality. Austria might argue that since she had become a member of the UN she might be disposed to argue should the case arise that her neutrality position still held and entitled her to refuse to participate in any joint action under the Charter. It was largely because the Swiss realised that this argument would not be a sound one that they had not sought to join the UN. Should the position have had arisen in which under the Charter there did evolve upon a neutral State an obligation to participate in joint military action, Article 103 of the Charter would unquestionably cause the Charter obligation to prevail. However under Article 43 of the Charter no State is under any actual obligation (in the absence of military agreement) to take any specific military action or provide forces – so the situation was unlikely to arise. It was agreed, therefore, by the Four Powers that Austrian neutrality would be armed neutrality. By the end of the year practically all States with whom Austria had diplomatic relations had agreed to recognise her neutrality. Austria's international position among the nations was confirmed on 14th December when she was admitted to membership of the United Nations.

There was one notable omission from the messages of congratulations which poured into Vienna. The Federal Chancellor of the German Republic, Dr Adenauer, made an unfriendly reference to Austria's attitude towards the Hitler régime and recalled his Federal German representative from Vienna on "long leave". The problem which was resolved before the end of the year, involved the provision of the treaty debarring the Austrian Government from returning German assets to their former German owners except in cases where the property did not exceed 260,000 Austrian Schillings (about $13,000).

On the 19th of June, Harold Macmillan moved the Second Reading of the Austrian State Treaty Bill in the House of Commons and by 5.30 pm it had gone through all stages. All four Allied Powers had ratified the treaty by the 27th July and it therefore came into effect. In accordance with the provisions of the treaty, all occupying forces were therefore required to evacuate Austria within 90 days of this date, which made the deadline midnight on the 25th October. The 26th October would be recognised thereafter as a national holiday.

History will record that the occupation of Austria had been a difficult albeit necessary undertaking both for the Austrians and for the British and other occupying Powers. By 1955 Austria was developing into a prosperous and politically stable country and perhaps for that reason alone the occupying Powers could take some of the credit. But like all occupying Powers in history they had overstayed their welcome.

The British left behind no memorials but history would record that their influence had been a far greater gift and of far more value to Austria. They would be remembered especially in the British Zone for their compassion, understanding and ungrudging help during the dark days of 1945 and for saving Carinthia for Austria.

They were last to enter Austria in 1945 and it was arranged that they should be the last to leave in 1955. Their small remaining detachment left Klagenfurt on 25th October a few hours before the midnight deadline by way of 8th May Strasse, so named to commemorate their arrival and the end of hostilities in Europe. They proceeded along the route by which they had come under very different circumstances ten years before, through Velden, Villach and Val Canale . . .

Soon they were gone and Austria was free.

10

EPILOGUE

When the flags of the Four Allied Powers were lowered for the last time in Vienna, it was to herald a new epoch for Austria. Two hundred and eleven months of military occupation came to an end, an occupation which started with Hitler's "historic mission" and ended with a nod from Moscow. We shall never know for certain how and why Russia decided to quit Austria and as late as December 1954 many were resigned to a partitioned country. It was indeed fortunate that the reversal in Soviet policy came when it did for a year later the Hungarian uprising would undoubtedly have stiffened Russian opposition to an Austrian treaty. In the end the stubborn resistance and patience of the Western Powers paid off and Austria's future was assured.

Since independence, the country has developed into one of the most prosperous in Europe. It is true this would not have been possible without the early goodwill of the Western Powers, especially from the United States through the Marshall Plan. In 1947 the United States Government voted some $4,000 million for the European Recovery Programme (ERP). Between 1945 and 1955 Austria received $1,600 million of ERP aid of which nearly 90 per cent was contributed by the United States. It must also be admitted that Austria's neutrality at times has appeared precariously balanced without the strength of NATO but this danger has never deterred her progress, especially in the international community.

In 1956 Austria joined the Council of Europe, and a year later the International Atomic Energy Agency (IAEA) was established in Vienna. In 1960 she joined the European Free Trade Association (EFTA). Her army joined UN peace keeping forces in the Congo in 1960, Cyprus in 1964 and the Middle East in 1968. The Organisation of Petroleum Exporting Countries (OPEC) was established in Vienna in 1965, and two years later the United Nations Industrial Development Organisation (UNIDO). A free trade agreement was signed with the EEC in 1972. To enlarge Austria's international cooperation programme the UN City was completed in Vienna in 1979.

In the dark days of November 1940, when Britain stood alone against the might of the Third Reich, Winston Churchill in a speech at the Mansion House stated Britain's policy towards Austria when he said that Austria was one of the countries for whom "we have drawn the sword and for whom our victory will supply liberation". After a long and bitter struggle this promise had been fulfilled, but the price had been high. Before Alexander's armies had crossed the Austrian frontier, the British alone had lost over 45,000 men killed in action. The Commonwealth war cemeteries dotted around the Italian countryside are a grim reminder of those days. In Austria itself the 589 men of the British forces killed in action there, or who died on active service, lie at rest in a quiet corner of Carinthia overlooking the Wörthersee, a perpetual memorial to Austria's liberation.

The Commonwealth War Grave cemetery outside Klagenfurt where 589 men of the British forces killed in action in Austria, or who died in active service lie at rest.

BIBLIOGRAPHY

CHAPTER 1

PRO/F0371/46664
PRO/F0371/46616

	The Treaty of St Germain-en-Laye, 10th September 1919
	The Treaty of Versailles, 28th June 1919
Schuschnigg, Kurt von.	*Austrian Requiem*, Victor Gollancz, London, 1947
Gordon Brook Shepherd.	*Anschluss*, Macmillan, London, 1963
Neave, Airey.	*Nuremberg*, Hodder & Stoughton, London, 1978
Schlesinger, Arthur M. Jnr(Ed).	*The Dynamics of World Power Vol 1, Western Europe*, McGraw Hill, New York, 1973
Herzstein, Robert, Edwin.	*Waldheim: the missing years*, Grafton Books, London, 1988
	The Reading Evening Post, 11th March 1988

CHAPTER 2

Wadl, Wilhelm.	*Das Jahr 1945 in Kärnten*, Kärnten Landesarchiv, Klagenfurt, 1985
	The Times, 8th May, 12th Sept 1945
Hemingway, Ernest.	*A Farewell to Arms*, Charles Scriber's Sons, 1929

PRO/WO170/4337

PRO/FO371/46610
Wadl, Wilhelm.

op.cit.
US Army in World War II, 1943-45, The War Department, Washington DC, 1968

Ralph G. Martin

The Woman he loved: The story of the Duke and Duchess of Windsor, Simon & Schuster, New York, 1973
Memorandum of the Government of the Federal People's Republic of Yugoslavia on Slovene Carinthia, the Slovene frontier areas of Styria and the Croats of Burgenland, Belgrade, 1947

Dedijer, Vladimer.

The Battle Stalin Lost, 1948-1953, Spokesman, Nottingham, 1978
The Times, 15th May 1945
The Times, 22nd June 1945

PRO/FO371/46619
PRO/FO371/46664
PRO/FO371/46620
PRO/FO371/46615
PRO/FO371/46614
PRO/FO371/46621
PRO/FO371/46622
PRO/FO371/46624
PRO/FO371/46617

New York Times, 31st July 1945

CHAPTER 3

PRO/FO371/46610

The Treaty of London, 26th April 1915

Macmillan, Harold.

Tides of Fortune, Macmillan, London, 1969

178

Wadl, Wilhelm.   op.cit.
The Times, 21st May 1945

PRO/FO371/46612

The Times, 24th December 1946

Tolstoy, Nikolai.   ***The Minister and the Massacres***, Century Hutchinson, London, 1986

Macmillan, Harold.   ***War Diaries***, Macmillan, London, 1984

Longworth, Philip.   ***The Cossacks***, Constable, London, 1969

CHAPTER 4

PRO/FO371/46682

Dedijer, Vladimir.   op.cit.

Egon Millonig.   ***Carinthia***, Wilhelm Andermann Verlag, Munich: 1960 (French and European Publications Inc., Rockefeller Center, New York)

Memorandum of the Government of the Federal People's Republic of Jugoslavia, op. cit.

Wambaugh, Sarah.   ***Plebiscites since the World War***, Carnegie Endowment for International Peace, Washington, 1933

Jessop, T.E.   ***The Treaty of Versailles: Was it just?***, Thomas Nelson & Sons Ltd, London, 1942

Wutte, Martin.   ***Freiheitskampf, 1918-1920***, VGK, Klagenfurt, 1922

PRO/FO371/46682

Memorandum No.1, Concerning the definite recognition of the pre-war boundary between Austria and Yugoslavia based on the Treaty of St Germain (1919) and the results of the plebiscite in Kärnten (1920), 12th September 1945

	Memorandum No.2, Concerning the impracticability of the Drau Frontier claimed by Yugoslavia, 1st October 1945
Langer, Robert.	*Memorandum on Yugoslav territorial claims against Austria, prepared for the Government of Yugoslavia*, New York, 1949
Herzstein, Robert Edwin.	op.cit.
	The Italian Peace Treaty, 1947
	The Austrian State Treaty, 1955

CHAPTER 5

	Memorandum of the Government of the Federal People's Republic of Yugoslavia, op.cit.
PRO/FO371/46616	
PRO/FO371/46610	
PRO/FO371/46593	
Beevor, J.J.	*SOE Recollections and Reflections 1940/45*, Bodley Head, London, 1981
Gordon Brook Shepherd.	*The Austrian Odyssey*, Macmillan, London, 1957
Howarth, Patrick.	*Undercover*, Routledge and Kegan Paul, London, 1980
Barker, Elizabeth.	***Churchill and Eden at War***, Macmillan, London, 1978
Lambie, Major J.C.	***Private Communication***, 1987

CHAPTER 6

	United States Army in World War II, op.cit.
PRO/FO371/46610	
	Annual Register of World Events, 1945, Longman Green, London, 1946

PRO/FO371/46617

The Times, 9th August 1945, 14th May, 17th May, 1st June, 8th August, 1946

Agreement concerning Control Machinery and Zones of Occupation in Austria and the Administration of the City of Vienna, London, 4th July 1945, 9th July 1945 and Vienna 28th June 1946 Cmd 6953 HMSO

PRO/FO371/46619

Your lifetime in pictures, New York, 1951

Handbook of Austria, issued by HQ, British Troops in Austria, 1948

Bader, William B.   ***Austria between East and West, 1945-55***, Stanford University Press, Stanford, California, 1966

CHAPTER 7

PRO/FO371/46610
PRO/FO371/46612
PRO/FO371/46613
PRO/FO371/46690

The Times, 26th April and 13th December 1946

Wadl, Wilhelm.   op.cit.

CHAPTER 8

PRO/FO371/46610
PRO/FO371/46612
PRO/FO371/46613
PRO/FO371/46690

Wadl, Wilhelm.	*The Times*, 22nd March, 26th April, 9th July, 13th Dec 1946 op.cit. *BBC Radio Four: File on Four* (presented by Liz Donnelly), 20th May 1986 *The Daily Express*, 3rd May 1986, 26th, 27th Feb 1987
Bower, Tom.	*The Paperclip Conspiracy*, Grafton Books, London, 1988 *The International Herald Tribune*, 6th May 1987 *The Sunday Mirror*, 8th February 1987 *The Daily Telegraph*, 3rd July 1987
Herzstein, Robert, Edwin.	op.cit.

CHAPTER 9

Macmillan, Harold.	*Tides of Fortune*, op.cit.
General Mark Clark.	*Calculated Risk*, George Harrap, London, 1951
Eden, Anthony.	*Full Circle*, Cassells, London, 1960
Bullock, Alan.	*Ernest Bevin, Foreign Secretary 1945-51*, Heineman, London, 1983
Dedijer, Vladimer.	op.cit. *The Times Summary*, 16th April, 16th May 1955 *The Austrian State Treaty*, 1955
PRO/FO371/117816	*Annual Register of World Events*, Longman Green, London, 1955

CHAPTER 10

	Commonwealth War Graves Commission, private communication, 1987.

182

APPENDIX

CHRONOLOGY OF EVENTS

1938

12 February:	Hitler and Schuschnigg meet at Berchtesgaden
11 March:	Schuschnigg postpones plebiscite arranged for Sunday 13 March
	Austrian cabinet resigns:
	Seyss-Inquart appointed Chancellor:
	Hitler closes German-Austrian border
12 March:	German troops invade Austria:
	Hitler arrives in Linz; makes his headquarters in Hotel Weinzinger
13 March:	Anschluss declared in Vienna:
	Hitler signs Anschluss in Linz at midnight
14 March:	Hitler arrives in Vienna
10 April:	Hitler's plebiscite gains 99.75% majority

1941

6 April:	Hitler visits Klagenfurt
14 August:	Churchill and Roosevelt announce the Atlantic Charter

1943

1 November: Moscow Declaration on Austria

1945

29 March:	Soviet troops cross the Austrian frontier in Burgenland
6-13 April:	Battle for Vienna
28 April:	United States troops cross Austrian frontier at Vils in Tirol
29 April:	French troops enter Vorarlberg
2 May:	German Army Group C in North Italy and Western Austria capitulates
	Marshal Tito orders his army to march on Austria and take Carinthia
3 May:	Klagenfurt and Villach declared open towns if SS units decide to defend Carinthia against British advance
7 May:	First British troops cross Austrian frontier at Kötschach-Mauthen:
	Gauleiter of Carinthia resigns
8 May:	British troops enter Klagenfurt at 9.30 am:
	Yugoslav troops enter Klagenfurt at 12 noon
	Tito proclaims the Anschluss of Carinthia with Greater Yugoslavia:
	Second World War in Europe ends at midnight
12 May:	British Military Government arrive in Klagenfurt
13 May:	Harold Macmillan flies to Klagenfurt to meet General Keightley
19 May:	Yugoslav troops retreat from Carinthia on a midnight deadline

3-13 June:	Allied Military Mission visits Vienna
4 July:	First Allied Control Council for Austria meets in London
9 July:	Zones of Occupation for Austria designated
17 July-2 August:	Potsdam Conference
24 July:	Soviet troops evacuate Styria: British troops enter Graz
1 September:	British, French and United States troops enter Vienna and take up zones of occupation
2 September:	Japan capitulates; end of Second World War
11 September:	First meeting of Allied Commanders in Chief in Vienna
1 October:	Austrian schools reopen
25 November:	General Election; first free elections since 1934
19 December:	First democratically elected Government formed
20 December:	Karl Renner becomes first President: Leopold Figl becomes first Chancellor

1946

5 September:	Austro-Italian Agreement on South Tirol

1947

10 February:	Italian Peace Treaty
16 September:	State of war between Britain and Austria officially terminated

1948

5 April:	Stained glass window dedicated to British Troops in Austria in Christ Church Vienna
12-14 June:	Field Marshal Montgomery visits British Troops in Austria
19 December:	St Stephan's Cathedral reopened

1949

3 May:	Austrian Government dedicate national memorial at Mauthausen Concentration Camp

1950

6 October:	Exchange rate for tourists increased to 72 Austrian schillings to £1
31 December:	Karl Renner dies

1951

1 June:	Population census gives population of Austria as 6,918,952
12 November:	British, American and French Legations in Austria raised to Embassies

1952

7 May: Leopold Figl received by Her Majesty the Queen in Buckingham Palace

18 July: Austrian Government approves seven Bills providing large scale amnesty for former Nazis and compensation for victims of Nazism

23 September: Anthony Eden visits Austria

12 December: Cultural agreement signed between Britain and Austria

31 December: Tourist traffic in Austria in 1952 reaches the million mark for the first time

1953

30 October: Tenth anniversary of the Moscow Declaration marked by 5 minutes stoppage of work in protest against Four Powers' failure to restore Austrian independence

1954

1 January: British forces in Austria reduced to one Battalion:

British waive all costs to Austria of the occupation amounting in 1953 to $2 million

9-14 July: Worst Danube flood since 16th century

1955

13 May: Harold Macmillan flies to Vienna to sign Austrian State Treaty

15 May:	Austrian State Treaty signed in Vienna; effective from midnight 25 October
25 October:	British troops leave Austria before midnight deadline
26 October:	National holiday proclaimed in Austria

TREATIES AND AGREEMENTS

1915	London Agreement
1919	Versailles
1919	St Germain-en-Laye
1920	Plebiscite in Carinthia
1920	Rapallo
1925	Locarno: Britain, France, Belgium, Germany, Italy
1934	Italy, France and Britain Agreement
1935	Italy, France and Britain Stresa Agreement
1936	Papen – Schuschnigg non-intervention Agreement

INDEX

Acheson, Dean, 121
Adolf Hitler Platz (Villach and Klagenfurt), 22
Alexander, Field Marshal (Supreme Allied Commander Mediterranean), 31, 36, 68, 159
Allied Commission, 117
Allied Control Machinery, 117
Allied Council, 117
Allied High Commissioners and Commander in Chiefs, 117
Allied Military Commissioners, 117
Allied Military Government, 13, 57, 117
Allied Military Mission to Slovenia, 91
Allied Powers, 13
Alpenfestung Alpine redoubt, 54
Altenmarkt in Pongau, 94
Altonburrow, sgt, 29
Anglo-Austrian Society, 97
Anschluss, 13, 21, 25, 26, 27, 35, 45, 60, 76, 98, 110, 141, 149, 150, 159, 164, 165
American 7th Army, 94
Auschwitz, 19, 152
Austria, customs and traditions, 130
    declaration of neutrality, 165, 171
    aid from European Recovery Programme, 175
    memorandums to British Military Government, 81
    on Russian front, 164
    political systems, 15
    resistance fighters, 88
    tourist trade 1948, 134
    Zones of occupation, 37
    map of, 33
Austrian State Treaty 1955, 69
    signing of, 167
    rights of Slovene and Croat minorities, 170
    transit facilities, 82, 85
Austro-Hungarian Empire, 56, 78

Barba, Yugoslav News Agency, 71, 72
Barbie, Klaus, 157
Battle Axe Division (Eighth Army), 29
Bavaria, 81, 85
BDM (Bund Deutscher Mädel), 143, 147
Behenbach, 61
Bela Garda (White Guards), 39
Belgrade Radio, 62
Belvedere Palace, 113, 167
Berchtesgaden, 17, 20, 85, 123
Berghof, 17
Beljak (Villach), 71
   see also Villach,
Belsen, concentration camp, 19
Belzec, concentration camp, 46
Berlin, 24
   Conference 1954, 164
Bevin, Ernest, 76, 161, 162, 168
   correspondence with Renner, 51
Biedermann, Major, 90
Bleiburg, massacre, 67, 82
Borman, Martin, 145
Brenner Pass, 90
British Military Government (BMG), 38, 41, 63, 125
   Press release, 72
British aid to Austria, 116
BTA (British Troops in Austria), 34, 47, 121
   strength, 122, 124, 166
   cost, 122
   organisation, 124
   sports, 128
   officers shops, 129
   postal services, 129
   hospitals, 133
   schools, 133
   relations with Austrians, 138
   civilian tasks by Royal Engineers, 136
   dedication of stained glass window, 138
   evacuation of, 173
Bulgarian troops, 39

Bundesregierung (National Government), 32
Burgenland, 81
Burgenland Croats, 56
Byrnes, James F., 161

Canal Valley, Kanaltal, see Val Canale
Carinthia, 31, 34, 53, 57, 61, 63, 64, 67, 68, 70-72, 81-83, 86, 87
    ceding of, 54, 78, 83
    census of German & Slovene speakers, 84
    Memorandums, 81
    Military zone, 53
    Provisional Government (Landesregierung), 32, 38
    Reichsgau, 87
    territorial claim by Yugoslavia, 54, 75, 78, 83
Carniola (Krain), 78, 87
Caserta, Allied Forces Headquarters, Italy, 34, 68, 89
Celovec (Klagenfurt), 53, 70, 71
    see also Klagenfurt
Censorship, 42
Census statistics, Carinthia, 79
    map of, 80
Chequers, 68
Chetniks, 39, 65, 69
Churchill, Sir Winston, 43, 68, 97, 98, 114, 176
Clark, Mark, General (Commander 15th Army Group), 159
Colditz, Oflag IVC, 94
Concentration camps, 19, 21, 45, 147, 152, 157
Cossacks, 30, 39, 65
Croats, 39, 65
    Minorities clause in Austrian State Treaty 1955, 170
Curfew, 41
Czernowitz (Cernovcy), 81

Dachau, concentration camp, 19, 94, 151
Dedijer, Vladimir, 162
Demjanjuk, John, 157
Denazification, 73, 141
Displaced persons (DPs), 39

Dollfuss, Engelbert (Chancellor of Austria), 15, 16
Dönitz, Admiral Karl (Commander in Chief German Navy and successor to Hitler), 34, 145
Domanov, General, 66
Domobranci, 39
Doppelbesitz, 64
Drau (Drava) River, 53, 69, 75, 78, 79, 91, 93
Drau Valley, 59, 67, 69, 75
Dravograd (Unterdrauburg), 39, 78, 82

Eagle's Nest, 17
Eberl, Commandant of Treblinka, 46
Eden, Sir Anthony, 43, 114, 168
Edwards, Lt, 29
Eichmann, Karl Adolf (Chief of the Jewish Section of the Gestapo), 155
Eighth Army, 29, 35, 54, 60, 67, 105, 124
Eisenhower, Dwight, General, 42
El Alamein, 35
Emigrés, Russian, 65
England, 18
England, Spiel, 111
Epilogue, 175

Ferdinand, Franz, Archduke, 111
Ferlach, 39
Figl, Leopold (Chancellor of Austria), 150, 166
Fischer, Ernst (Minister of Education), 142
Food shortage & distribution, 38, 108, 115, 116
Frank, Anne, 19
Franckenstein, Sir George (Austrian Ambassador to Britain), 101
Franz Joseph, Emperor of Austria, 112, 119
Free Austria Movement, 97
Fraternisation, 42
France, 18, 38
French troops strength, 122
Führer, see Hitler
Fussen, 37

Gailtal (Zilska Valley), 53, 63
Galloway, General Sir Alexander (British High Commissioner and Commander in Chief), 120
Garrison Commanders, 124
Gauleiter, 17, 32, 45, 90, 143
Gerlitzen, 143
German assets in Austria, 159, 163, 172
German speaking population, 78
German troops (in the Drau Valley), 39
Gestapo (Geheimestaats Polizei), 32, 87, 90, 143, 145, 147
Glaise – Hortenau, 19
Globocnig, Odilo, 19, 45
Gloggnitz, 48
Göring, Herman (Reichsmarschall), 24, 98, 145
Gospa Sveta (Maria Saal), 38
Graz, 35, 82
   British enter, 43
Greater German Reich, 13, 90
Gruber, Karl (Austrian Foreign Minister), 83

Habsburg, Charles, Archduke, 97
Habsburg, Felix, Archduke, 97, 99
Habsburg, Otto, Archduke, 97, 98, 99
Habsburg, Robert, Archduke, 97, 99
   Report to Foreign Office, 99
   Letter to Prime Minister, 101
Habsburg, Rudolf, 97
Harwich, 123
Harmel, Major General, 31
Heiligengeistplatz, Klagenfurt, 32
Heldenplatz, Vienna, 21
Hemingway, Ernest, 31
Hesketh – Pritchard, 91
Hess, Rudolf, 145
Heydrich, Reinhard (Head of SS Security – RSHA), 19
Hitler, Adolf, 13, 14, 15, 17, 20, 24, 27, 66, 86, 135, 147, 156, 175
Hitler salute banned, 145
Hitler visits Villach and Klagenfurt, 147

Hitler Youth, 112, 143
Hofburg Palace, 21, 168
Hook of Holland transit camp, 123
Hohenburg, Duke of, 111
Horst Wessel Lied, 18
    banned, 144
Hüber, Göring's brother in law, 19
Hungarian troops, 39
Hurd, Douglas, 156
Huth, Captain, 90

Idrija, 93
Inquart, Seys, see Seys – Inquart
Isonzo River, 31
Italian Partisans, 87
Italian Peace Treaty, 1947, 85
Italy, 30, 69, 78, 156

Jews, 19, 21, 152, 154, 157
    Statue in the Albertina Platz Vienna, 22
Julian Alps, 54

Kaes, Ferdinand, 90
Kaltenbrunner, Ernst (Chief of Gestapo – succeeding Heydrich in 1941), 19, 46, 88, 145
Kardelj, 162
Karawanken range, 54, 78
Kärnten, see Carinthia
Keightley, General Sir Charles (Commander Fifth Corps), 57, 65, 69
Keppler (Hitlers Commissioner for Austrian affairs), 19, 46
Kesselring, Field Marshal Albrecht, 136, 164
Klagenfurt, 31, 34, 38, 40, 42, 47, 53, 56, 68, 99, 101, 124, 129, 133, 135, 166, 173
    bombing of, 127
Klausner, Major Franz, 19, 45, 46
Koeszeg, 105
Kononov, Colonel, 66

Körner, Theodor (President of Austria), 168
Kötschach – Mauten, 29
Kramer, Joseph, 145
Krasnov, General, 66
Kreisky, Bruno, 153, 154, 155
Kristallnacht, 21
Krushchev, Nikita S., 69, 169

Lambie, Major J.C., 91, 92, 94, 95
Lancers, 31
Lech River, 37
Leningrad, siege of, 106
Leutschach, 56
Ley, Robert, 145
Lienz, 30, 54, 67
Linnas, Karl, 157
Ljubljana Gap, 105
Ljubljana (Laibach), 70
Löhr, General Alexander von, 32, 40, 83
London Treaty Conferences, 83, 162
Lublin, 46

Machold, Reinhard, 44
Macmillan, Harold (later Lord Stockton), 56, 65, 68, 166, 167, 168
Maier – Kaibitsch, 91
Malenkov, 163
Maria Saal, 38, 61
Maria Worth, 143
Maribor (Marburg), 82
Marogna-Redwitz, Colonel Court, 89
Marshall (General George C) Plan, 175
Mauthausen, 19, 94, 111, 145
May 8th Strasse, 173
McCreery, General Sir Richard (British High Commissioner and Commander in Chief), 119, 124
Medloc C, BTA troop train, 122
Memorandums from Carinthian Provisional Government, 81
Miestal (Mies Valley), 78

Molotov, Vyachesler, 162, 164, 167
Morgan (General Sir William) Line, 61
    map, 55
Moscow Conference, 1947, 161
Moscow Declaration, 14, 15, 162
Murray, Major General Sir Horatius (commanding Sixth Armoured Division), 31

NAAFI, 123, 127, 128
Napoleon Bonaparte, 85, 119
NATO, 165, 171, 175
Nazi(s) (National Socialist Party – NSDAP), 13, 17-26, 32, 43, 45-49, 52, 57, 82, 163
    amnesty by new Austrian Laws, 151
    banned, 144
    denazification, 109, 110, 141
    in Austria, 14, 26, 142, 154
    in Britain, 156
    in Styria, 76
    in U.S. Zone, 99, 100
    in Soviet Zone, 149
    purge of, 142
    teaching in schools, 146
    war crimes, 150, 151, 157
    war criminals, 145, 151, 152, 157, 158
    in the U.S., 156
Nürnberg trials, 145

Occupation, zones, 37, 117
Oflags, 39, 94
05 Resistance Group, 88, 109
Ostmark, 21
Ötztal, 89, 90

Pannwitz, General Helmut von, 66, 69
Papen, Franz von (former German Chancellor, Minister in Vienna, later German Vice Chancellor), 19, 145

Paper clip conspiracy, 155
Park Hotel Villach, 47
Partisans, 30, 38, 39, 60, 61, 70, 87, 91, 93, 95, 96
    engagements with enemy in Carinthia & Styria, 95, 96
Partition, 14, 160
Patton, General George, 112
Peck, Colonel Capel, 79
Piesch, Hans (Landeshauptmann of Carinthia), 83
Pinay, M., 167, 168, 169
Plebiscite, Carinthia 1920, 14, 79, 84, 86
    proposed by Schuschnigg for Sunday 13th March 1938, 20, 26
    Salzburg 1921, 81
    Tirol 1921, 81
    Vorarlberg 1919, 81
    Burgenland 1921, 81
    Map, 80
Plöcken Pass, 29, 67
Political systems, 15
Pörtschach, 124
Post Hotel, Villach, 47
Pravda, Soviet News Agency, 71
Proclamations, British & Yugoslav, 53, 57
Prohibited Frontier Zone (PFZ), 63, 70
Pula (Pola), 61

Raab, Julius (Chancellor of Austria), 163, 166
Radkersburg, 56
RAF, 93, 94, 96, 101
Railway, via Marburg-Graz, 82
Rainer, Friedrich (Nazi Gauleiter of Carinthia), 17, 32, 34, 45, 46, 73, 141
Rapallo, Treaty of, 56, 78
Rape, of women in Vienna, 105
Rashke, Lt, 90
Reder, Walter, 152
Renner, Karl (President of Austria), 27, 32, 47-52, 78, 86
    letter from Stalin, 51
    correspondence with Bevin, 51
    arrested by US Military Police, 52

Stalin's telegram to Soviet Commander, 50
Reparations, claimed by Soviet Union, 159, 163, 164
　　　claimed by Yugoslavia, 56
Resistance, 87
　　　Austrians executed, 88
Rhineland, 17, 18
Ribbentrap, Joachim von (German Foreign Minister), 24, 145
Rifle Brigade, 31
Rimini, 69
Roosevelt, Franklin D., 43
Rosenbach, 63, 70
Rosental, 39
Rumanian troops, 39
Russian Zone, tour of, 111

SA (Sturm-Abteilungen), 143, 145
Sabotage in Carinthia, 88, 93-96
Salzburg, 17, 26, 34, 37, 81, 85, 99, 123, 170
Sarajevo, 111
Saualpe, 91
Sauerwein, Hubert, 89, 90
Schmidt, Guido (Austrian Foreign Minister), 19
Schönbrunn Palace, 113, 119, 124, 168, 169
Schuschnigg, Kurt von (Chancellor of Austria), 17, 18, 25, 26, 27
Schwammberger, Josef, 158
Schwarzenberg Palace, 113
Scottish POW Camp, 69
SD (Sicherheitsdienst), 143, 145
Seeland (Yzerko), 64, 78
Seys – Inquart, Arthur (Reich Commissar for the Netherlands and
　　　designated Foreign Minister in Hitler's Will), 19, 45, 145
Shkuro, General Andrei (Kuban Cossack leader), 66, 69
Slovene(s), 56, 60, 63, 65, 70-75, 79, 82, 84, 85, 86, 90
　　　Carinthia, 75, 90
　　　language in Carinthia, 75
　　　Minorities clauses in Austrian State Treaty 1955, 170
　　　National Liberation Committee, 72
　　　Partisans, see Partisans
Slovenski Procevalec, Yugoslav News Agency, 71

Sobibor, 19, 46
Soboth, 56
SOE, 111
Sopron, 81
South Tirol, 79, 85
Soviet Union, agreement to sign Austrian State Treaty 1955, 165
    Germans ordered to leave Russian Zone, 149
    Memorial in the Schwarzenbergplatz, 139
    population lost in war, 106
    reparations claimed from Austria, 159, 164, 165
    troops strength, 122, 166, 167
Spittal, 142
SS (Schutz-staffeln), 19, 31, 34, 69, 71, 93, 143, 145
Stalag VIII, 39, 94
Stalin, Marshal Joseph, 43, 50, 65, 70, 114, 121, 163
Stalingrad, 35, 110
St Florian, 113
St Germain, Treaty of 1919, 17, 56, 78, 79, 81
St Paul, 95
St Stephens Cathedral (Stefanskirche), 112, 168
Studeny, Franz, 89
Styria, 35, 37, 43, 44, 64, 75, 95
Sud Banhof, bomb damage, 113
Swastika, 17, 21, 144
Switzerland, 81, 85, 166, 171
Szokoll, Major, 89, 90

Tanjug, Jugoslav News Agency, 70
Tarvisio, 31, 54, 95
Tass, Soviet News Agency, 71
Tauschitz, Stefan (Deputy Landeshauptmann), 32
Third Reich, 13, 82, 158
Three Powers, 13, 37
Tirol, 37, 90
see also South Tirol
Tito, Marshal Josip Broz, 31, 34, 45, 54, 61, 68, 71, 121, 162, 163
    Partisan army, 59
    reparations claims on Austria, 54
    territorial claims on Austria, 54, 56, 57, 75, 78, 81, 83

Tolbukhin, Marshal Feodor Ivanovich (Commander Third
   Ukrainian Front), 35, 56, 58, 65, 90, 112, 114, 115
Tolmezzo, 30, 67
Tolstoy, Nickolai, 65, 67, 69, 70
Treblinka, 46, 157
Trieste, 29, 31, 57, 122, 163
   map of Trieste & Venezia Giulia, 55
Truman, Harry S., 114

Uiberreither, Siegfried (Nazi Gauleiter of Styria), 46
Ukrainian Front, Third, Soviet Troops of, 50, 105
Ukrainians, in Carinthia, 40
UN Charter and Austrian neutrality, 171
United States, aid to Austria, 115, 117, 175
UNRRA, 115
Unterdrauburg, see Dravograd,
US Fifth Army, 105
US Sixth Army, 105
US 101st Airborne Division, 95
USSR, see Soviet Union and Russia,
Ustasi, 39, 69
US troops, strength of, 122

Val Canale, Canal Valley, Kanaltal, 29, 34, 54, 78, 85, 173
VE day, 34
Velden, 67, 79, 173
Venezia Giulia, 56, 57, 61, 63
   map of, 55
Venice, 57
Versailles, Treaty of, 17, 81
Vienna, bomb damage, 112
   Burg Theatre, 113
   Commander BTA, 124
   daily ration, 116
   dedication of BTA windows in Christ Church, 138
   dedication of Soviet memorial in Schwarzenbergplatz, 139
   Nazi Police, 16
   Districts of Allied occupation, 117

(map of), 118
Fall of, 105
Opera House, 113
Rape statistics, 105
Viktring, 67
Villach, 31, 36, 54, 63, 71, 78, 93, 94, 96, 99, 122, 124, 134, 135, 173
  bombing of, 127
Villacher Strasse, Klagenfurt, 32
Vils, 37
Voitsberg, 35
Volkermarkt, 38, 64
Volkssturm, 107
Von Braun, Werner, 156
Vorarlberg, 37, 81
Vyshinski, 163

Waldheim, Kurt (President of Austria), 15, 83, 152, 153, 154
Wallinger, Sir Geoffrey (British Ambassador), 166
War crimes, see denazification
Watch List (US), 153
Weir, General Steven (Commander Forty Sixth Infantry Division), 43
Weissenfels, 78
Welsh Guards, 67
Werwolf (organization), 143, 144
Wiener Neustadt, 111
Wiesenthal, Simon, 69, 151, 155, 157
Windisch, 75
Windsor, The Duke and Duchess of, 26
Winterton, General Sir John (British High Commissioner and
  Commander in Chief), 114, 115, 120
World Jewish Congress, 152, 156, 158
Wörthersee, 47, 53, 176
Würzburg, 105

Yalta, 37, 38, 65
Yugoslavia, 31, 39, 53, 56, 57, 60, 62, 63, 68, 78, 81-85, 87
  Army, 57, 59, 60
  Austrian Memorandums on territorial claims, 81

border incidents, 138
expelled from Cominform, 161, 162
illegal frontier crossings, 63, 64
Institute, Klagenfurt, 170
Nazi invasion, 87
PFZ, 63, 70
reparations from Austria, 54, 56
territorial claims on Carinthia, 38, 54

Zones of occupation, 37, 117